**CAMBRIDGE
EXAMINATIONS
PUBLISHING**

CAE
Writing Skills

Felicity O'Dell

CAMBRIDGE
UNIVERSITY PRESS

PUBLISHED BY THE PRESS SYNDICATE OF THE UNIVERSITY OF CAMBRIDGE
The Pitt Building, Trumpington Street, Cambridge, United Kingdom

CAMBRIDGE UNIVERSITY PRESS
The Edinburgh Building, Cambridge CB2 2RU, UK
40 West 20th Street, New York, NY 10011–4211, USA
10 Stamford Road, Oakleigh, VIC 3166, Australia
Ruiz de Alarcón 13, 28014 Madrid, Spain
Dock House, The Waterfront, Cape Town 8001, South Africa

http://www.cambridge.org

First published 1996
Third printing 2001

Printed in the United Kingdom at the University Press, Cambridge

ISBN 0 521 46646 6

Contents

Map of the book

Unit	Text type	Sub-skill	Language focus	Vocabulary work
1	Overview	Getting to know the exam	Being accurate	Vocabulary relating to writing exams
2	Writing based on a reading task	Planning and organising	Being polite and tactful	Using your own words
3	Letters	Who are you writing to?	Varying the style – formal and informal	Phrasal verbs and their formal equivalents
4	Articles	Openings	Emphasising	Avoiding dull words
5	Narratives	Content	Telling stories	Vivid verbs
6	Reports	Paragraphs	Presenting ideas effectively	Linking words and expressions
7	Writing about work	Endings	Making connections	Vocabulary of work
8	Notes, notices and announcements	Punctuation and spelling	Being brief, clear and precise	Commonly confused words
9	Instructions and directions	Clarifying	Varying sentence structure	Choosing the best word
10	Reviews	Writing with style	Giving opinions	Positive and negative words
11	Brochures	Correcting your work	Promoting and publicising	Idioms
12	Competition entries	Performing well on the day of the exam	Showing a range	Using words accurately and appropriately

To the student

About the exam

The Certificate in Advanced English (CAE) is for students at an advanced level of English. Many students taking the exam have already gained a grade C or higher in the Cambridge First Certificate in English exam. However, this is not essential if you want to take the CAE.

There are five papers in the exam: Reading (Paper 1), Writing (Paper 2), English in Use (Paper 3), Listening (Paper 4) and Speaking (Paper 5). This book helps you prepare for Writing (Paper 2). You may like to use *CAE Reading Skills* and *CAE Listening and Speaking Skills* to help you prepare for Papers 1, 4 and 5.

Paper 2 (Writing) takes two hours. You have to answer two questions – one compulsory question and one other question from a choice of four. In all, you are expected to write about 500 words, 250 for each of your two answers.

In order to get good marks in Paper 2, you must be able to write accurately in English. However, you must also show that you can answer the question in an appropriate way; you must organise your answer well and what you say must be to the point and in a suitable style.

In some ways, the Writing Paper in CAE tests your reading skills as well as your writing skills. It is very important that you read the questions carefully and that you do exactly what is asked of you.

About this book

For many CAE candidates, Paper 2 is the most difficult paper in the exam. Working with this book will give you practice in all the skills you need in order to get good marks in this part of the exam. The book prepares you for the kinds of questions which you may be asked and tells you exactly what examiners are looking for when they mark your work. You are also given plenty of carefully guided practice in answering exam-type questions.

However, the writing skills which are practised in the book are not just useful for the exam. Planning a piece of writing, organising its content effectively and presenting ideas in the most appropriate ways are all skills which lead to better writing outside the exam room as well as inside it.

Good luck with *CAE Writing Skills*, and good luck with the exam!

Felicity O'Dell

To the teacher

Aims

CAE Writing Skills aims to help you prepare your candidates for Paper 2 (Writing) of the Certificate in Advanced English (CAE). Our principal aim is to provide systematic coverage of the specific skills needed for the Writing paper of the exam. However, the intention of CAE Paper 2 is to test candidates' ability to write the kinds of texts which people are most likely to need to write in everyday life; thus, the writing skills practised in this book are skills which are useful for any advanced learners wishing to improve their ability to write in English. The book can, therefore, be used with a group of advanced learners who are not taking the exam.

CAE Writing Skills is primarily intended for class use as it is felt that candidates will benefit from discussing many of the issues related to writing well with each other. However, most of the activities could be carried out by a student working in self-study mode and a full key is provided at the end of the book.

Many candidates do less well in CAE Paper 2 than they do in other parts of the exam. This book pays particular attention to those aspects of performance which lead to lower marks – failure to read the task carefully enough or to grasp its implications, poorly planned and organised work, careless presentation.

Organisation

The book is divided into twelve units. The first of these provides an introduction to CAE Paper 2, giving information about what kinds of tasks the exam may include and about what examiners are looking for when they mark candidates' work. The other eleven units all address one particular task type tested in the exam. The final unit includes an overview of the exam-specific work of the book.

Each unit begins with a selection of exam-type tasks so that students know what sort of task they are working towards. Usually a unit then has an awareness-raising discussion activity, focusing attention on the task type in question. Later exercises work on details of language use, leading up to gradually more extended pieces of writing. The final task of each unit involves writing an answer to one or more of the initial tasks. In the more detailed language work, each unit focuses on one sub-skill of writing, one aspect of vocabulary work and one area of language use. The Map of the book indicates exactly which language areas are covered in each unit.

The work on these aspects of language, while discussed in the context of the task addressed by the unit as a whole, is relevant to the development of writing skills as a whole. It is, therefore, recommended that students should work through all the units in the book even if they wish to spend more time on some task types than others. It is not, however, necessary to work through the units in the order in which they are presented. While it makes most sense to do Unit 1 first and Unit 12 last, the remaining units can be done in any order that suits your candidates' programme of studies.

Suggestions for use

The range of language areas worked on in each unit provides for lessons with some variety of pace and activity type. Clearly, class time can be saved if some of the activities are set as homework; extended writing tasks are particularly suitable for this.

An interesting way of extending the work on any given task type is by bringing in examples of writing in that genre for students to look at as part of the awareness-raising activities; students can identify, for example, what 'real' writers do to make an article or a brochure interesting. While it is clearly useful if these examples are in English, monolingual classes may also benefit from looking at texts in their own language and discussing with their teacher the extent to which the techniques employed are also used in English texts of a similar type.

It is certainly recommended that some time in class be spent with students in pairs or small groups looking at and discussing each other's first drafts of work, followed by rewriting at home in the light of these classroom discussions – though, obviously, this needs to be organised with some sensitivity.

It is also felt that students will learn most effectively if the teacher merely indicates where an error has been made in written work and encourages students to work out how to correct their work themselves.

These processes help to train the critical eye, which will enable students to produce their best work in exam conditions.

The most important pieces of advice in the book are highlighted as Exam or Study tips. It is a good idea to focus attention on these in class. Ask students why they think a particular tip has been emphasised, enquire about the extent to which they already follow this advice and discuss methods of implementing the advice.

Above all, it is hoped that teachers and students will find this book both enjoyable and useful. While the principal aim is for candidates to do their best in CAE Paper 2, it is also hoped that working with this book may make writing outside the exam room an easier and more agreeable task.

Felicity O'Dell

1

Foundation unit

The aim of this unit is to answer the following questions.

- What does CAE Paper 2 consist of?
- How is it marked?

You will:

- practise vocabulary useful for talking about written work.
- practise an effective method of error correction.

The unit aims to show you precisely what kind of writing you can be asked to do in CAE Paper 2. It tells you what the examiners are looking for as they mark your work. In this way you will set off with a basic understanding of the exam which will help you to get the best marks you can.

What does CAE Paper 2 consist of?

1 ☞ Can you already answer these questions about CAE Paper 2? If not, find the answers in the text below.

1 How long does the paper last?
2 How many questions do you have to answer?
3 How many words are you expected to write?
4 Is there a choice of questions?
5 Are any of the questions worth more marks than other questions?

The CAE Writing Paper takes two hours. It is divided into two sections, each of which gets a mark out of ten. In Section A you are required to produce one or more pieces of writing (approximately 250 words in all) in response to quite a long reading text (or texts). You can only do well in this section if you have read the text(s) carefully and do exactly what the task requires you to do. There is no choice in Section A. In Section B you have to write one piece of approximately 250 words and you can choose from four tasks.

The official description or Specifications of the CAE Writing Paper lists the following tasks as the kinds of things you may be asked to write.

articles (newspaper, magazine)   leaflets   notices   announcements
personal notes and messages   formal and informal letters   reports
reviews   instructions   directions

Note that sometimes exam questions use different words like memo, account or brochure to describe what you have to write.

The exam, therefore, aims to ask you to write the kinds of things which one day you might need to write in English.

2 Look at the list of text types in activity 1 again and complete the table.

Text types	Have you ever written one of these in your own language?	Have you ever written one of these in English?	Do you think you ever might need to write one of these in English?
articles (newspaper, magazine)			
leaflets			
notices			
announcements			
personal notes and messages			
formal and informal letters			
reports			
reviews			
instructions			
directions			

The Specifications also point out that each task set in the exam will be provided with:

- a precise context or setting for the piece of writing.
- a clear statement of the reason why such a piece of writing is to be written.
- a clear statement of who the intended readers of the piece are.

3 ⚏ On the following pages you have an example of a typical CAE Paper 2. Look at the tasks carefully and complete the table below. In the first column you should choose one of the ten text types from activity 2. Some parts of the table have already been completed to help you.

Task	Kind of writing	Purpose of writing	Intended readership
Section A, task i	article		
Section A, task ii		to invite members to meeting, to encourage them to bring ideas	
Section B, task 1			editors selecting new reviewers; also, indirectly, magazine readers
Section B, task 2		to publicise company	
Section B, task 3			
Section B, task 4	report		

You are the secretary of your local English language club. The club meets once every fortnight and its aim is to provide interesting activities to help members practise their English. The committee is anxious to organise the kinds of events during the coming year that members would most like. With this in mind, the committee has carried out a survey of members' opinions and it is also planning to hold a meeting to discuss the proposed programme of events.

Read:
    the table showing the results of the survey of members' opinions.
    a memo from the chairperson of the committee to you as secretary of the club.

Question	Yes	No	Not sure
Are you satisfied with the current club programme?	5%	75%	20%
Would you like more visiting speakers?	58%	15%	27%
Would you like more discussions?	45%	18%	37%
Would you like more social events – parties, English food evenings, barbecues etc?	87%	5%	8%
Would you like the club to organise concerts, drama events etc?	76%	9%	15%
Would you take part in such shows?	54%	19%	27%
Does the club need more members?	85%	2%	13%
Could you help with fund-raising activities?	63%	34%	3%
What kinds of visiting speakers would you like us to invite?	– talks on UK, USA, Australia, Canada etc. with slides; talks about and readings from English novelists, poets; talks on social and political issues		
What kinds of discussion events would you like us to organise?	– topical issues; one member prepares talk on controversial subject of own choice and starts off discussion; discussion about films, short stories etc.		
Ideas for fund-raising activities	– concerts open to public; films open to public; discos; bring and buy sale; providing English-tutoring agency for schoolchildren etc.		

English Club Members' Opinion Survey: 73 members from a total membership of 98 replied to the questionnaire.

> **MEMO**
>
> The survey was really useful and we've been able to draw up a
> good programme for next year, I think. We'd like to organise a
> meeting as soon as possible for all the members to discuss what
> we're proposing - do you think you could send round a note
> inviting people to something on Saturday week, usual place, 8
> to 10 p.m. (tea and biscuits). By that time they should've read
> your article on the survey in the newsletter so they'll know
> the background to our proposals. At that meeting we'd also like
> to organise our campaign for new members so people should come
> with ideas.
>
> See you soon.
>   L.

Now write:

i) an article for the club newsletter reporting the results of the opinion poll of members. (Write about 200 words.)

ii) a note to be sent to all club members in accordance with the chairperson's instructions. (Write about 50 words.)

SECTION B

Choose ONE of the following writing tasks. Your answer should follow exactly the instructions given. Write approximately 250 words.

1

World Monthly is a rapidly expanding international magazine. We are looking for people from a range of countries to join our panel of book and film reviewers. Interested applicants are requested to send us a sample review of any two contrasting books they have read or films they have seen recently. The review should be about 250 words long. It should indicate what the books or films are about and should also make it clear what the reviewer's opinion of each of the works considered is.

You decide to apply to join the panel of reviewers. Write the review which you would send to the magazine as a sample of your work.

2 The company which you work for would like to raise its international profile and has invited you to write a publicity brochure aimed particularly at young people in other countries. Your brief is to give clear basic information about the company and its activities. You should also indicate ways in which the work of the company might be of interest to young people perhaps as users of its products or services and/or as potential future employees. Write the brochure.

3 This is part of a letter which you receive from an Australian penfriend of yours.

> ... It was great to get your last letter with all your news. I feel as if I know you and your family quite well now and wonder if we'll ever actually meet one day. When you next write, I'd be really grateful if you could help me with a school project. We've been asked to find out about wedding customs in other countries – what kind of ceremony takes place, what people eat, what they wear, any special traditions, that sort of thing. The more information you can think of, the better, of course.

Write your reply.

4 Last weekend you and a friend went on a three-day course at a sports centre some distance from your home. You were supposed to spend the days learning a new sport and the nights in a luxury hotel. However, there were a number of problems with the weekend – concerning both the accommodation and the sports training. You rang the company organising the holiday to complain and they asked you to send in a detailed report informing them exactly what the problems were and explaining what you feel they should do about the situation. Write your report.

How is CAE Paper 2 marked?

Every CAE Paper 2 answer is marked by two examiners, each of whom independently gives the work a mark out of 5. On the following pages you have an example of the mark-scheme which examiners use.

4 ☛ A puzzled student has annotated the mark-scheme with some question marks to indicate points that he or she does not fully understand. Work with a partner and discuss the places the student has questioned. Can you help explain? Then compare your answers with those of other students in the class.

CAE Paper 2: general impression mark-scheme

An impression mark out of 5 is awarded to each composition. Examiners are assessing language and task achievement.

?

?

The **general impression mark-scheme** is used in conjunction with a **task-specific mark-scheme** which focuses on criteria specific to each particular task, including relevance, length, omissions, specific language / vocabulary, and layout. (Following the conventions of writing letters, reports etc. is part of task achievement.)

Poor handwriting, spelling errors or faulty punctuation are not specifically penalised but the overall impression mark will be affected if communication is impeded. Allowances are made for appropriate colloquialisms and American usage / spelling.

The criteria for assessment with reference to the general impression mark-scheme are summarised as follows.

5	Totally positive effect on target reader; minimal errors, resourceful, controlled and natural use of language, showing good range of vocabulary and structure. Completion of task; good use of cohesive devices, consistently appropriate register. No relevant omissions.	**?**
4	Sufficiently natural, errors only when more complex language attempted. Some evidence of range of vocabulary and structure. Good attempt at task, only minor omissions. Attention paid to organisation and cohesion; register not always natural but positive effect on target reader achieved.	**?** **?**
3	Accuracy of language satisfactory; adequate range of vocabulary and structures; reasonable task achievement. Or an ambitious attempt at task, with a good range of vocabulary and structures, causing a number of non-impeding errors. There may be minor omissions but content clearly organised. Would have a positive effect on the target reader.	**?** **?**
2	Errors sometimes obscure communication and / or language is too elementary. Some attempt at task but notable omissions and / or lack of organisation and cohesion would have negative effect on reader.	
1	Serious lack of control and / or frequent basic errors. Narrow range of language. Totally inadequate attempt at task.	
0	Not enough comprehensible language for assessment.	

5 🔑 Can you now answer these questions about the general impression mark-scheme?

1 If a candidate has left out an important part of the answer, what is the maximum mark which he or she can get?
2 If it is impossible to read a piece of work, what mark will it get?
3 Must a candidate make no mistakes to get 5 marks?
4 Apart from accuracy, what two things characterise the vocabulary and structures used in a band 5 piece of writing?

5 Do candidates have to pay attention to the organisation of their writing to get 3 marks?

6 What are the 'conventions' of writing a formal letter?

CAE Paper 2: task-specific mark-scheme

As well as looking at the general impression mark-scheme markers also use a mark-scheme which is specific to the particular task being marked. This makes specific comments relating to the following aspects of a task:

1 content
2 organisation and cohesion
3 range
4 register
5 target reader
6 accuracy

Here is an example of a specific mark-scheme relating to Section B, task 1 from the sample paper in this unit. The comments describe the kind of work typically expected from a good student.

Content	Review of two books / films. The two clearly contrast. The review (a) outlines the content and (b) comments on each work.
Organisation and cohesion	The review opens in a way likely to catch the reader's attention. It also finishes on a strong note. The books or films under review are clearly named early on in the article and there is never any doubt which one the writer is referring to.
Range	Evidence of range in the language used for comparing and contrasting as well as in that used to describe the books or films and to comment on them.
Register	Neutral.
Target reader	The reader will be clear about the nature of the works being discussed and the writer's opinion of them. The reader will also find the review interesting to read.
Accuracy	No mistakes except when more difficult language is attempted. No mistakes that would confuse the reader.

6 ⟳ The six points listed in the specific mark-scheme above lead the examiners to ask themselves a number of questions as they read a student's work. Match the questions below with points 1–6 above.

a) Has the student used an appropriately formal or informal style?

b) Have all the parts of the question been answered?

c) Would the reader be appropriately informed or interested?

d) Does the writer use a good variety of words, expressions and structures?

e) Has the candidate made many mistakes? Do the mistakes affect the meaning of the writing?

f) Has the answer been well planned and do the sentences and paragraphs link together well?

7 ◦−◦ Here are two examples of students' work in answer to tasks from the sample paper. One of these candidates got 5 marks and one got 3 marks. Consider the questions listed in activity 6 and decide which piece of work got which mark. Why do you think they got these marks?

A

Following our telephone conversation this morning, I am sending in a full report about the 3-day course at your sports centre from which I have just returned. I have been going on such short sports courses for over three years now and never in all this time have I spent such a disagreeable time.

Accommodation

My troubles started at the hotel where my friend and I were obliged to wait for over an hour for the key to our room. No sooner had we got into our room than we realised that the bathroom taps were dripping. To make matters worse we were only able to get cold water even though the plumber spent at least two hours every day in our bathroom attempting to repair the system.

We were, then, taken completely by surprise when we realised that we had to buy food for ourselves despite having been previously informed that the cost of the course included all meals.

Sports training.

The sports training was far from what was advertised. We even had to book places in the swimming pool because its use was restricted. Free instruction was very limited too and there was an extra charge for any individual attention. I must also complain about the punctuality of the instructors. On one occasion we were obliged to wait for as much as half an hour before the instructor turned up in the morning. I was, moreover, dissatisfied with the quality of the instruction which I received.

Suggestions

I should like to suggest that you carry out an immediate check on the hotel where you accommodate people attending your courses with a view perhaps to changing to more reliable accommodation. Most importantly of all, you should make sure that your trainers are themselves well-trained and provide good standards of instruction. Personally, I should appreciate some kind of compensation for being misled by your publicity.

B

Hello Andrew,

Thank you very much for your letter that I've recently received from you. I'm writing to tell you about wedding customs in Belgium. Myself, I'm going to marry next year and it's a great pleasure to give you some information.

There are a lot of things to do before the marriage. One of this is to have a look at what you could need in your household to receive it as a present from your friends. You choose what you would like to have and the shop will make up a list of these things. Everyone who want to make a gift for the wedding can now claim to have a look at this list and choose which one he would like to give.

A ceremony a few days before the wedding happens is a meeting between the bridegroom and his friends to have a party the last time they can do this only under men. Naturally, it's just a joke that they meet each other the last time.

On the celebration day the bridegroom will see the bride's dress the very first time. Usually she wears a wonderful white robe which is such a lovely look. The bridegroom wears a dark suit. The ceremony happens in a church if they both marry the first time. If not, they would marry only at a registry office and without these beautiful dresses.

After the ceremony, the invited people and the whole family from the bride-couple will meet each other in a restaurant where they'll have dinner until after midnight. When the couple return to their house or flat something won't be as it was before. It's possible that they cannot go into the bedroom because the door cannot be opened.

I hope al this will help you to manage a good school project. I'm looking forward to hear about it.

Many greetings,

Writing accurately

STUDY TIP

It is important that you write as accurately as possible. Your teacher may point out your mistakes to you. He or she may correct your mistakes himself or herself or use a correction code to indicate the type of mistake you have made. But your teacher will not be able to help you in the exam. Get used to rereading everything you write and looking for mistakes. Check especially for mistakes you know you often make.

8 🔑 It is important that you write as accurately as possible. A student has made a number of mistakes in the following piece of writing. The teacher has underlined the mistakes and has indicated what kind of mistakes have been made, using the code in the box below. Can you correct these mistakes, using the teacher's comments to help you?

Sp.	Spelling	WO	Word order
WW	Wrong word	Pr.	Preposition
T	Tense	VF	Verb form
Ag.	Agreement (e.g. singular subject with singular verb, plural subject with plural verb)	RW/WF	Right word, wrong form

VF I have can swim ever since I have been a small child and people says T / Ag

I am a very good swimmer. Most of all I enjoy to swim on the sea. VF: Pr

T Most weekends I'm going to the beach which is about 30 kilometres far from my home. One day when I WW

Pr: arrived to this beach it was so

RW/WF crowdy that I decided to walk further along the beach than

RW/WF usually. Soon I came to a delightfull little cove that was surprising Sp / RW/WF

deserted. I saw a sign who said Ag

'For naturists only' and I thought that meant the beach was for only WO

nature-lovers.

Planning and writing

9 Choose one of the tasks from Section B of the sample paper at the beginning of the unit and write an answer. Then ask your teacher to mark your work.

Use your teacher's comments on your work and write out an improved version. Then give your work to your teacher for checking.

2

Writing based on a reading task

The aim of this unit is to answer the following questions.
- What kind of writing tasks based on reading might CAE Section A ask you to do?
- What is the importance of the reading input and how should you use it?
- Should you change given text into your own words?
- How can you be polite and tactful in English?
- How can you best plan and organise a piece of writing?

CAE Paper 2 tests your ability to read as well as to write. All the questions in CAE Paper 2 require you to read the questions very carefully and to think about the implications of their wording before you write your answer. This is particularly important in Section A.

In Section A, you have quite a lot to read – possibly as much as 400 words – and you cannot get good marks unless you show that you have thoroughly read and fully understood the point of what you have read. However, care is taken that what you have to read is not too difficult; you will not be expected to understand anything as hard as the reading texts in Paper 1.

Outside the exam room too, you often base your writing on something you have read. For example, you write an essay for a teacher based on a book you have read; you write a letter in response to one you have received from someone else; you write a report for your boss summarising information you have noted down from different sources; you write to a newspaper or magazine commenting on one of its articles. The work practised in this unit is, thus, useful not only for the exam but also for more general writing work.

In this unit we shall look back at Section A from the sample paper on pages 7–9. We shall also consider the following two examples of rather different types of Section A tasks.

1 Last month you spent some time in England. You took part in a very enjoyable and useful one-month summer school and stayed with an English friend. Your friend now sends you a letter with an enclosed cutting from the local newspaper, describing the summer school. There are a lot of mistakes in the newspaper cutting and your friend has made some notes on these. Read the letter and the cutting with your friend's notes and then write a letter to the newspaper editor as suggested by your friend.

Thanks very much for your letter. I'm so glad you enjoyed your stay here. I do hope you'll be able to come again next year. But, unfortunately, it looks as if next year's summer school may not be happening!

I thought you might be interested to see this cutting. There are so many mistakes - only the first paragraph looks okay to me! I've marked all the mistakes I found but I suppose there may be more. Why don't you write to the editor and complain? It would be a pity if the future of the summer school was put at risk because of this sort of rubbishy report.

Let me know what you do.

Love and best wishes,

Chris

Summer School disapointing

THIS SUMMER Canchester was to welcome a hundred young people from all over the world to take part in a new international summer school combining English language studies with a range of arts and sporting events. It was hoped that the school would become an annual Canchester event.

Unfortunately it was a disaster from beginning to end. It was hardly international since three-quarters of the participants came from the same country! It was hardly a school since only one of the five teachers was actually a qualified language teacher and few of the participants actually wanted to spend time in the classroom. Even the word 'summer' could be said to be misleading since it rained almost every day of the month our visitors were here.

The arts events were few and far between – there were a couple of films, a photographic exhibition and an evening of rather childish entertainment put on by the participants. Although local people were invited to all these events, few found them attractive enough to attend. The sports events were more successful, particularly the football, table-tennis and swimming competitions. Unfortunately, the football aroused so much enthusiasm that there was a rather unpleasant fight at the final where one Swedish participant's leg got broken.

One typical participant (Ana, 24, Mexico) told me, 'The summer school was a waste of time and money. I don't think they should try to organise a summer school in Canchester again next year.' We agree with her.

Handwritten annotations:

Not true, is it? Thought max. no from any 1 country was 10 from yr country - not a problem, was it?

Far more than 5, surely.

Thought only JG was unqualified?

You even asked for extra evng. classes!

What about weekly concerts, drama group, video club?

It was not childish!!!

I went to everything along w. 50 or so others!

J. broke his leg in an accident not a fight!

Was there an Ana from Mexico in the group? I don't remember her.

2 You are the secretary of your local English club, which is planning to help pay for one person to go and study in the USA for three months. A large number of people applied, the best were interviewed and the list has been narrowed down to four. The chairperson of the club committee has asked you to make the final decision and to write a report to the committee explaining why you felt your first choice was more suitable than the others.

Read the background information about the short-listed candidates provided in the table, the notes made after these candidates were interviewed and the chairperson's memo to you. Then write:

i) your report to the committee as requested by the chairperson. (Write about 200 words.)
ii) a letter to one of the unsuccessful applicants informing him or her of the committee's decision. (Write about 50 words.)

In your writing you may add details but should not change any of the facts presented.

Short-listed candidates

Applicant	Age	Occupation	Aim of study trip	Comments
A.S.	20	Student (of Eng.)	To practise Eng. first on course, then working on summer camp with children	Wants to be primary school teacher; parents unemployed
T.R.	65	Retired nurse	To study medical Eng.	Wants to do translating; has given great service to local community; widow
D.O.	24	Mechanic	To do business course	Plans to set up own business. Married with one child (spouse at home)
S.M.	30	Univ. lecturer, teaches students of Interpreting	To do research into the modern American language	Working for doctorate; highly praised scholar; excellent teacher

Notes after interviews

A.S. Shy but intelligent. Never been abroad. English not so good.

T.R. Very keen to go. English good. Own health not perfect.

D.O. Ambitious and enthusiastic. Dirty fingernails! Taught himself Eng. (to good level).

S.M. Very impressive. Has been to US 4 times before. If goes, wd. write series of reports for club newsletter from US.

Chairperson's memo

... *So we'll leave it up to you to make the final choice. I don't envy you. They're all good in their own way – just wish we could fund the lot! When you've chosen, write a short report telling us why you selected who you did as opposed to the other candidates. Then, if you wouldn't mind, write to one of the unsuccessful candidates explaining the situation.*

All the best,

J

1 ⌕–0 In the previous unit, you analysed questions according to the categories in the table below. The suggested answers for the Section A sample tasks in Unit 1 are included here as a reminder. Analyse tasks 1 and 2 from the beginning of this unit in the same way.

Task	Kind of writing	Purpose of writing	Intended readership
Unit 1; Section A, task i	article	to report on opinion survey results, to inform readers	members of local English club
Unit 1, Section A, task ii	note	to invite members to meeting, to encourage them to bring ideas	members of local English club
Unit 2, task 1			
Unit 2, task 2 i			
Unit 2, task 2 ii			

EXAM TIP

Remember to read all CAE writing tasks very carefully before you start writing. This is particularly important in Section A of the paper where your writing is based on a reading task.

2 🔑 Look again at the Section A questions analysed in activity 1 and tick all the bits of information which it would be relevant to include in each case. The first task has been done for you as an example.

Unit 1, Section A, task i

- the fact that the club meets every fortnight
  (information already known to readers)

- the precise percentages for every question asked in the survey
  (too specific)

- description of main ideas suggested   ✓

- description of some of the disastrous events that have taken place at club meetings recently   *(not relevant, already known)*

- statement of aims of club   *(not relevant, already known)*

- outline of trends shown by the survey   ✓

- description of what the club is   *(already known to readers)*

- brief statement of further action likely to be taken as result of survey   ✓

- precise details of next year's programme   *(not yet decided)*

- brief statement of details of survey – its purpose, numbers responding etc.   ✓

It will probably not be relevant to include any of the points on the list which have not been ticked.

Unit 1, Section A, task ii

- details regarding time and place of the meeting
- the fact that there will be tea and biscuits
- summary of article
- statement of aims of meeting
- reminder to bring proposals for next year's programme to be discussed at meeting
- reminder to bring ideas about new members' campaign to meeting

Unit 2, task 1

- correction of all the mistakes in the article
- an accusation that the editor was lying
- request for a printed apology and correction of the mistakes
- statement of your nationality and fact that you took part on course
- description of what Canchester is like as a town for foreign visitors
- an outline of how one student broke his / her leg
- a hope that the summer school will continue in future years
- an attack on modern journalism

Unit 2, task 2 i

- name of person you chose
- statement that you could not make a choice and pass decision back to committee
- decision to split sponsorship money between all four candidates short-listed
- reasons favouring your choice
- weaknesses of three candidates not chosen
- greetings to fellow committee members
- strengths of three candidates not chosen

Unit 2, task 2 ii

- statement of problem regarding candidate's dress, e.g. dirty fingernails, at interview
- statement of who got the sponsorship
- expression of regret that sponsorship could not be offered to this candidate
- full explanation as to why successful candidate was chosen
- encouragement for applicant to try other sources for sponsorship

3 ☛ Work with a partner and discuss why you decided not to include some of the points listed in activity 2. Was it because the specific point was too general, too specific or not tactful? Was the information already known to readers? Or was it because the point was inappropriate for readers in some other way?

4 ☛ Work with a partner and decide which of the six points below were required in the three different Section A tasks you have been looking at. Note that there may well be more than one answer for each task. Then compare your answers with those of other students in the class.

1 using information from one reading text to correct errors in another
2 summarising information you read in the question
3 expanding notes
4 selecting a section of the reading text for especial comment and expansion
5 'translating' from formal to informal English or vice versa
6 being tactful in expressing a message that is 'difficult' in some way

Importance of reading input

The large reading input in CAE Paper 2 Section A is there for a purpose. Firstly, it serves to give you as much precise information as possible, not only about the purpose of writing and the intended readership but also about the content of what you have to write. This means that examiners can judge your work on your ability to handle English rather than your ability to write creatively or to imagine situations. It also means that candidates are doing exactly the same task.

5 🔑 **Work with a partner and discuss the following pieces of advice. On the basis of what you have read about Section A so far, do you think they are good pieces of advice? Why (not)? Then compare your answers with those of other students in the class.**

1 As the exam lasts two hours, it is a good idea to allow 70 minutes for Section A and 50 minutes for Section B.
2 Skim the task rather than spending time on small details.
3 Underline or highlight the important parts of the task.
4 Copy large chunks of the reading input in writing the answer.
5 Do Section B first and then Section A.
6 Check spellings of words in the reading input which you have used in your answer.

Using your own words

> **EXAM TIP**
>
> Although you can, of course, make use of words and expressions you read in the texts in the tasks it is advisable, as far as possible, to use your own words. This will make it clear both that you have fully understood the texts and that you have a range of English vocabulary and structures at your command.

6 🔑 **Below you have some sentences taken from answers to the three tasks from the beginning of this unit. The underlined words in each case come straight from the reading texts provided. Put the underlined words into your own words. Then compare your answers with those of other students in the class. How many alternatives did you find as a group?**

Example: *1 It would be regrettable if the future of the summer school was threatened by such an inaccurate and misleading article as this one.*

1 It would be a pity if the summer school was put at risk because of this sort of rubbishy report.
2 It is not true to say that arts events were few and far between.
3 It is unfair to suggest that few of the participants actually wanted to spend time in the classroom.
4 Some students even asked for extra evening classes.
5 TR has given great service to the local community.
6 SM is a highly praised scholar.
7 DO's spouse is at home looking after their one child.
8 AS gave the impression of being shy but intelligent.

Being polite and tactful

7 Work with three or four other students. Is it rude to address strangers and close friends in the same way when using the other languages known to members of your group?

8 ⚏ Complete the table with sentences which convey a similar message but in a different register. Some parts of the table have already been completed to help you.

Function	Writing to a close friend	Writing to a stranger
Thanking for present	Thanks for the great book – love the cartoons.	Thank you for the most enjoyable and amusing book you sent me.
Requesting a favour		I was wondering if there might be any chance of your giving me some assistance with a project I am currently working on?
Making a suggestion	How about meeting at the theatre next Saturday?	
Apologising	I'm terribly sorry I forgot to post you the report.	
Complaining		I would be very grateful if you could ensure that your sons turn their music down after 11 p.m.
Initial salutation		I hope that you and your family are keeping well.
Drawing letter to a close	Better go now or I'll miss the post. Longing to see you soon. Love,	

9 ⚓ Work with a partner and decide whether the following sentences are polite or tactful enough in answer to the questions indicated. If the answer is *no*, explain why this is the case. Then compare your answers with those of other students in the class.

1 Although a majority of club members are dissatisfied with the programme provided, few are actually prepared to make the effort to do much about it themselves.   (Unit 1, Section A, task i)
2 Remember we want you to bring along some rather more original ideas than you managed to come up with last time.   (Unit 1, Section A, task ii)
3 I have never read such a load of rubbish in my life!   (Unit 2, task 1)
4 If you do not print a full apology, you will soon be hearing from my lawyers.   (Unit 2, task 1)
5 You should stop publishing such lies.   (Unit 2, task 1)
6 I'm surprised that TR made it to the short-list.   (Unit 2, task 2 i)
7 You were really too old to be considered for our sponsorship. (Unit 2, task 2 ii)
8 SM was by far the best candidate at the interview stage.   (Unit 2, task 2 ii)

Planning and organisation

EXAM TIP

It is important to spend time reading the question very carefully. It is also important to allow time for planning your answer carefully so that you know the approximate form your answer will take before you begin to write it out fully. This is a much more effective use of time than writing your answer out once and then, as many students do in the exam, copying it out again in better handwriting.

How you write your plan is a matter of personal choice. You may make a numbered list of paragraph headings. You may note down your ideas as they come to you and then number them. You may prefer to do a diagram of some kind. It does not matter which method you choose. It is also quite likely that your plan will not be immediately comprehensible to another person. What is important is that your plan should help you get an overview of:

– what you have to write.
– how you can present it logically to the reader.

10 Here are three different ways of writing a plan for the article which students were asked to write in Unit 1, Section A. Work with a partner and decide which style of planning you prefer and why. Would you prefer to do your plan in a completely different style? If so, what style would you choose and why?

A   Introduction- outline of what survey consisted of
Summary of statistical results
Practical suggestions for events made
Fund-raising proposals
Conclusion – encouragement to attend new programme of meetings.

B   Summary of statistical results – focus on surprises in what was illustrated by results (e.g. more interest in social events than in visiting speakers or discussions)   2
Fund-raising proposals – why we need money and what we'll use it for as well as suggestions for getting money   4
Do come along to new style meetings   5
Aim and content of survey   1
Suggestions for future events – some of points from sheet + possible examples   3

C
statistics
why survey
what it told us   money
event ideas
COME ALONG!

11 Work with a partner and decide how you would organise your answer to one of the other Section A tasks you have been discussing in this unit. Write brief notes to outline the content of each paragraph. Compare your plans with those of another pair of students.

12 Choose one of the three Section A tasks you have been working on in this unit and write an answer.

EXAM TIP

As you read the exam question, highlight all the points you need to refer to in your answer. After writing your answer, tick all the points highlighted – to make sure you haven't forgotten anything.

3 Letters

The aim of this unit is to answer the following questions.

– What different kinds of letter might CAE ask you to write?

– How do formal, semi-formal and informal letters differ?

– How should your style vary depending on whom you are writing to?

– When are phrasal verbs appropriate in letters? Which ones might be most useful?

Letters are probably what you are most likely to have to write in English – both in the CAE exam and in 'real life'. There are, of course, many different types of letters.

The four tasks below show you some of the kinds of letters that you might be asked to write in CAE Paper 2.

1 You are the secretary of your college's English club. A professor visiting from the USA has written offering to give a talk to the club on Varieties of American Pronunciation. Your club needs speakers but you have heard that this professor tends to talk for too long and that his interest in pronunciation is rather specialised for your members. Write a reply. Accept his offer but tactfully suggest a programme that you feel will be more acceptable to your members. Offer overnight accommodation and give him some information about the club and its membership which will help him to prepare an appropriate talk.

2 This is part of a letter which you receive from a penfriend in the USA.

> We're doing a school project on sports and games in different countries and I'd be so grateful if you could help me. We're supposed to include sections on (a) sport in the school curriculum, (b) most popular participant and spectator sports for different ages and sexes, (c) any unusual traditional sports and games and (d) recent changes in sporting tastes and habits. I've already got information from a couple of penfriends in other countries and something about your country would mean I could hand in a really good piece of work for once!
>
> Best wishes
>
> Karen

Write a letter to Karen.

3 You read an article about your country in an English language magazine. The article makes you very angry because it recommends that tourists should not visit your country. The article also prints some other basic factual errors about your country. Write to the editor of the magazine correcting the mistakes and expressing your anger at the article.

4 This is part of a letter which you receive from a close friend of yours.

> In the summer some friends of mine are going to spend two months travelling in Australia and New Zealand. I'd really love to go with them and have already got enough money saved up. But my parents are set against it. They say I should stay at home and study for the university entrance exams I have to take next year. They then argue that I'd be better to keep my money for when I'm at university and living in a flat on my own. And then they add that it could be dangerous for three young people on their own. How can I persuade them that it would be a good idea for me to go?

Write your reply.

How do formal, semi-formal and informal letters differ?

Letters can be seen as being on a continuum from very formal to very informal. CAE Paper 2 will not ask you to write a specialised business letter requiring a professional knowledge of commercial words and expressions. However, you may be asked to write a formal, a semi-formal or an informal letter. How do you know what degree of formality is appropriate? What differences does the letter's place on the formal / informal continuum make to its content and style?

The degree of formality of a letter depends on:
- your relationship with the person you are writing to.
- the purpose of the letter.

- You write formal letters to someone whom you do not know or to whom you are in a subordinate position. The purpose of the letter is usually an impersonal or serious one.
- You write informal letters to someone whom you know well or with whom you are on equal terms. The purpose of writing is, often, personal; it may be light-hearted or it may be more serious.
- Semi-formal letters fall between these two extremes. They may be to someone much older or in a superior position to you but whom you know so well that you can relax the formality of your writing. They may be to someone whom you do not know well but who is the same age and level as you so that an extremely formal letter is inappropriate.

1 🔑 Look at the four tasks at the beginning of this unit. Put them in order from most formal to most informal.

2 Think about some of the letters you remember writing – in any language. Describe one or two letters to the class making clear who you were writing to and the purpose of writing, e.g. *close friend, to congratulate on new job*. Discuss the degree of formality which such letters would require in English.

3 🔑 Read the following letters and decide where they should be placed on a formal to informal continuum. Underline all the words and expressions which helped you find your answer. Then compare your answers with those of a partner.

A

> 14 Loudon Road,
> London
> NW6 3AL
>
> 21st September 1995
>
> 12 Loudon Road,
> London
> NW6 3AL
>
> Dear Mr and Mrs Winterspoon,
>
> It is with regret that this has to be my first letter to you as our new neighbours.
>
> Please would you be so kind as to dissuade your son from playing such loud music so late at night. My wife has long been prone to suffer from insomnia and it is quite intolerable for her to have to endure such a cacophony until one o'clock every morning. If your son insists on playing records until so late, could he not at least purchase headphones so that others are not inconvenienced?
>
> If your son does not refrain from such antisocial behaviour in the future, I shall have no choice but to contact the police.
>
> Yours sincerely,
>
> David Fogey

B

London,
21st Sept.

Darling Jo,
    Hope you had a great flight home, and are missing me as much as I miss you. You will write soon and tell me all you're getting up to, won't you?
    Things have been pretty grim here since you left. Just work and more work. I suppose the neighbours are glad at least that I don't have music on every evening any more.
    I'm moving ahead with plans to come and see you one weekend next month. If I book now, I can get a cheap flight for the second w/e in the month. Would that be OK for you? I really don't want to wait any longer to see you again.
    Drop me a line ASAP and I'll go ahead and book a flight if you just give me the word.
    All my love,
Chris
XXXX

Varying the style

TIP

Certain features of language, e.g. phrasal verbs, are more suitable for informal letters while other features, e.g. literary expressions, are more suitable for formal letters. Remember to vary your style of writing according to the degree of formality of the letter you are writing.

4 🔊 Work with a partner and decide which features of language below are typical of formal letters and which are typical of informal letters. (They might be found in semi-formal letters to a greater or lesser extent.)

phrasal verbs   literary expressions   colloquial vocabulary
the word *nice*   long sentences   full forms of verbs (*I would* etc.)
carefully constructed sentences and paragraphs
contractions (*I'd* etc.)   sentences that sound close to spoken English
sentences that are clearly written rather than spoken English
question tags   omission of subject of sentence

5 🔊 Work with a partner. First decide whether each sentence comes from a formal or an informal letter and underline any words or phrases that seem particularly characteristic of that style. Then write the same thing in the other style. You may also feel that it is appropriate to make slight alterations to the content of the sentence.

Example: *1 Thank you very much*. formal. *Thanks*. informal

1 Thank you very much for your letter of the 6th December.
2 I'm awfully sorry to have been slow in getting back to you but I've been dreadfully busy at work.
3 I should very much appreciate a reply at your earliest convenience.
4 I would be grateful if you could forward me some information about villas to rent on the Mediterranean coast.
5 How's life? I hope all's well with you these days.
6 She says he's a nice guy but I think she's off her head, don't you!
7 You may contact me by telephone at the above number.
8 OK if we pick you up at 6 and then we'll have time for a drink or two?

6 🔊 Here are the beginnings and endings of some sentences which you may find particularly useful when writing informal letters. Complete them in any appropriate way.

1 Thank you .... received yesterday.
2 It was lovely .... last weekend.
3 I hope we .... again soon.
4 I wish you .... here with me.
5 I'm sorry I .... a long time.
6 I must stop... catch the post.
7 Please .... your parents.
8 I'm looking forward .... soon.

7 🔊 Here are some sentences from more formal letters. Complete the sentences with one word only.

1 I am writing in .... to your advertisement in *The Times*.
2 I should like to .... for the position of tourist guide.
3 I would be .... to come for interview at any time convenient to you.
4 I should be .... if you could send me further information.
5 I .... a stamped addressed envelope with this letter.
6 I shall be sure to reply by .... of post.
7 I would be grateful for a reply at your earliest ....
8 Here are the names and addresses of two .... who have kindly agreed to answer any questions you may have.
9 I am writing with .... to the article on bicycle theft in yesterday's *Guardian*.
10 I trust you will be able to print a .... of the mistakes in the article within the next few days.

8 🔊 Imagine that Chris, the writer of the second letter in activity 3, wanted to write to an elderly friend of his parents who had just been to stay with his family and whom he was planning to visit soon. Such a letter would need a more formal style than that he wrote in activity 3. Write an appropriately formal letter. Then compare your letter with those of other students.

Phrasal verbs and their formal equivalents

As we saw above, phrasal verbs are most typical of informal letters – although there are some which have no more formal equivalents and are common in all types of letter (*look forward to*, for example). Most phrasal verbs, however, do have formal equivalents and these would be preferred in most formal letters whereas the formal equivalents would be very rarely used in an informal letter.

9 🔊 Work with a partner and discuss these sentences from some students' answers to task 1 at the beginning of this unit. All the sentences are rather too informal in style. One way of improving them would be to rewrite them using formal equivalents for the phrasal verbs the students chose. Use a dictionary if necessary. You may need to make other alterations to the structures in the sentences.

1 I am so glad you have been talked into giving a lecture to our members next month.
2 The club meeting room has been recently done up and so should be a pleasant venue for your lecture.
3 As our village is rather cut off, perhaps we could arrange for you to be put up overnight with one of our members.

4 I think you will find that the breakfast which Mrs Hunt will give you will make up for the inconvenience of having to stay overnight.

5 I was sorry to hear that you felt you were coming down with flu and hope that you will have got over it by the time of the meeting.

6 Some people told me off last year for setting up talks which were too long as most members feel quite done in at the end of a long day's work and so prefer talks to be reasonably short.

7 I hope you won't be put out if I ask you to keep your talk down to 45 minutes.

8 I understand that you have recently brought out a book on your travels throughout the English-speaking world.

9 Perhaps your talk could look at some of the linguistic insights which you picked up on your travels.

10 ⚲ Other students attempted task 4 and were, conversely, too formal in their choice of register. Can you make the sentences below rather less formal by replacing the verbs in italics with phrasal verbs which have an equivalent meaning? Use the verbs in brackets at the end of each sentence. Remember that you may again need to make other changes to the structures used in the sentences.

1 I've been *postponing* replying to you until I had *pondered* your questions fully. (put, think)

2 It may be hard to *dissuade* your parents *from* wanting you to stay at home. (talk)

3 Make sure you regularly *raise* the point that travel is well-known for broadening the mind. (bring)

4 There is no point in *pretending* that you will spend most of your time in Australia in libraries. (make)

5 You should make it clear that you will *persist with* your studies even though you are abroad. (carry / go)

6 *Support* your promises with some concrete statements about how you intend to *fulfil* your plans. (back, carry)

Planning and writing

11 ⚲ Look again at the four tasks at the beginning of this unit. Plan an answer for each of these tasks – you will probably need to write four to six paragraphs. Write a plan for each of your letters in the form of four to six paragraph headings. Then compare your plans with those of other students in the class.

12 Write one of the letters you discussed in activity 11.

Articles

This unit is going to work on features of articles in general. The next unit will look at the specific characteristics of writing a narrative, which is a type of article often used in CAE.

Here are four CAE-type tasks requiring you to write articles.

1 Your school or college has organised a month's programme of evening and weekend activities for students – films, discussion groups and talks from visiting speakers, among other things. You have been asked to write an article for the school or college newsletter in which you both tell students what activities have been arranged and try to encourage your readers to attend the activities.

2 An international magazine asks you to contribute an article recommending the area where you live – or another region that you know well – as a suitable place for honeymooning visitors from abroad. You should describe the area and make a range of suggestions about places they can go and activities they might enjoy during their holiday.

3 While you are on holiday in a foreign country, you meet some students from a local university and you start discussing current problems in both countries. They ask you to write an article for their university newspaper dealing with one of these problems and making some suggestions as to how you feel the problem should be dealt with.

4 You subscribe to an English-language magazine which is specially for people interested in your own favourite sport / hobby. You decide to submit an article to this magazine in which you describe an amusing experience which you had when practising this hobby / sport.

1 ⟲ Look at the four exam tasks. Work with a partner and discuss how to complete the table. The first task has been analysed for you as an example.

Task	What is the aim of the article?	What do you know about the likely readers of the article?
1	to inform / advertise	fellow students – are all at the same college; could take part in the activities college is organising; are probably interested in meeting other students; probably have little spare money
2		
3		
4		

What's special about articles?

In the previous unit we worked on letters. You almost certainly have far more experience of writing letters – both in English and in your own language – than you do of writing articles. It can be useful to compare the skill of letter-writing with that of article-writing.

2 ⌐o Read the outline below of the special characteristics of articles. Complete the notes on the next page about how writing an article compares with the more familiar task of writing a letter.

Articles, like letters, can be written in a formal or an informal style – it all depends who you are writing for. Writing an article, however, is in other ways rather different from writing a letter.

When you write a letter, you usually know the person you are writing to and so you can feel confident about what you have to explain in your letter and about what there is no need to say. Moreover, you can be fairly sure that the person you send your letter to will be interested enough to read it to the end, regardless of how interesting or entertaining your letter may or may not be.

When you write an article, on the other hand, you may know roughly who you are writing for – you can guess something about the kinds of people likely to read any particular magazine or newspaper – but your potential readers will probably vary quite considerably one from the other in terms of their background experience and knowledge. You, therefore, have to write in such a way that your article is appropriate for a variety of people. Finally, you cannot be sure that your readers will finish your article. They may not even start reading it if the title or opening paragraph does not catch their eye. If they do not find it interesting or well-written, they will certainly not read it to the end.

> Similarity between writing an article and a letter: ....
>
> Contrasts between readers of letters and articles:
>
> Readers of letters: Readers of articles:
>
> i)..........................   ....
>
> ii)..........................   ....
>
> iii)..........................   ....
>
> This means that an article should:
>
> i) ....
>
> ii) ....

Attracting and holding readers' attention

3 How can article-writers attract and keep the attention of their readers? Work with one or two other students and list as many ways as you can. If possible, look at some English-language magazines and newspapers of articles in general CAE coursebooks to help you collect ideas. Write brief headings to remind you of your ideas. Compare your ideas with those of other students. Add any other ideas to your list.

EXAM TIP

Bear in mind the following ideas for attracting and holding readers' attention.

1 Think up an eye-catching title for your article.

2 It is particularly important that your first paragraph should make the readers want to read on.

3 Make sure that each paragraph has a distinct topic and that there is a clear progression from one paragraph to the next.

4 Every now and then ask the readers a question.

5 Avoid boring words like *nice*, *good*, *get* and *bad*.

6 Express yourself in an emphatic rather than a dull way. (You might even want to exaggerate a little.)

7 At least sometimes, use direct rather than reported speech.

8 Illustrate your points with examples rather than just making general statements.

9 Vary the length of your sentences.

10 Try to create brief pictures in words of what you are describing so that the readers can see in their mind's eye the person or place you are writing about.

11 Surprise or interest the readers by sharing some unexpected or particularly significant fact(s) with them.

12 Making contrasts can be a very effective device in an article. Refer, for instance, to two places, people or situations which are very different from each other.

13 Address your readers in the second person, i.e. calling them *you*.

14 Bring the article to an effective close by referring in the last paragraph to something mentioned earlier in the article.

4 Work with a partner. Did you think of all the ideas in the exam tip box? Discuss which you think are the six most important ideas.

5 🔊 Read the article below. Which techniques has the writer used to hold readers' attention?

HONEYMOON UNDER CAPRICORN

The perfect place for that once-in-a-lifetime (hopefully) dreamtime? How about a thousand miles east of Africa, under Capricorn[1], on a sugar-and-spice island that dips its toes in the Indian Ocean? An island where casuarina pines[2] sway across white talcum powder sand and a coral reef keeps the sharks at a safe distance. Where the people are charming, the service in the hotels irreproachable and the food is terrific. If this is your idea of a honeymoon base, then go to Mauritius. After no less than five visits, it's still one of my favourite islands.

From somewhere few people in the west had heard of 18 years ago, Mauritius has become a prize destination in the brochures. Tourism has been a tremendous boost to the island's economy and the capital, Port Louis, has grown from a dusty old port into a sprawling commercial centre, but elsewhere the island's beauty spots remain unspoilt.

Most of the hotels are in splendid isolation or little groups. You wake up in the morning not to the sound of traffic but to the musical notes of the little red cardinals or bull-bulls[3] who later sneak beakfuls of sugar from the breakfast tables.

Choose the old-colonial graciousness of the St. Geran. Princess Caroline of Monaco sleeps here and so does Frederick Forsyth[4]. One of his short stories is set in this hotel.

The beach is a step across the coarse, tropical grass of its well-watered lawns. And there's enough going on by day (watersports, tennis, golf) and night (Sega dancing[5], well-honed cabarets and barbecues by the shore) to keep you amused should you never want to step outside the perimeters of the hotel. But what a waste to go all that way and not see something of such an enchanting island! Hire a moke[6] and drive up to Black River Gorge among its strange pointed mountains or across the tea plantations of the Plaine Champagne. Visit Pamplemousses Gardens where Pierre Poivre discovered pepper, or play Hemingway[7] for a day and go deep-sea fishing. This is one of the world's best areas to catch the big marlin and yellow-fish tuna[8].

But save that Frederick Forsyth story until you're back at home. You'll see why when you read *The Emperor* in *No Comebacks*.

---

1 refers to Tropic of Capricorn, an imaginary line around the earth 23.5° south of the Equator
2 a kind of tree
3 two kinds of bird
4 contemporary writer of thrillers
5 type of dancing that was fashionable when the article was written
6 basic open car
7 Ernest Hemingway, US writer (1899–1961). The reference here is to his novel *The Old Man and the Sea*, which is about deep-sea fishing.
8 two kinds of fish

Opening paragraphs

6 🔑 Match the titles of eight articles (A–H) with their opening paragraphs (1–8).

A Last resort for the Mediterranean
B A flexible society that would let us work, rest and play
C Jungle stories
D Chorus of disapproval for English curriculum
E Early Autumn Heat Wave
F Motherhood past midnight
G How a writer turned teacher
H Is there money in lost memories?

1 Ever considered setting up your own sure, instant, further education college at home? Ever been to a learning workshop? The best ones are short sharp shockers – over and done with in a day.

2 A revised English curriculum that sets specific targets for 'correct' standard English and a list of recommended literature, was met by a barrage of professional protest yesterday.

3 In 1907, Lt. Col. Percy Fawcett of the Royal Artillery was surveying a remote area of the Brazilian Amazon. While many parts of the Amazon remain hardly explored today, the world's largest tropical basin – 2.7 million square miles – was still almost completely unknown to westerners at the time and Fawcett was one of its first modern explorers.

4 It's 11 p.m. in the 'DNA lounge', a nightspot in downtown San Francisco. A group of young professionals arrives and begins filing through a small door at the end of an upstairs balcony. Emerging with thick, fruity drinks, they quickly disappear into the swelling crowd downstairs. On the other side of the door is a small brightly coloured room and the Smart Bar, which sells an enigmatic selection of 'nutrient cocktails' and 'cognition-enhancing' pills: Razzo Blast, X-tras, Party Pilz and, for a special 'mental and sensory charge', Smart Navel.

5 I grew up with a workaholic father who likes to get a day's work done before other people have breakfast and a mother who juggled a full-time academic career with knitting sweaters for her four children. Having just completed a study on the benefits of part-time work I am guiltily aware that – just like my parents – my partner and I work long hours in demanding jobs and see too little of our children.

6 It is mid-September, the temperature is steady in the high seventies and low eighties. Every morning at six thirty the sun has already set the tone for another sunny, warm day with a slight breeze off the sea to make the heat pleasant. What shall we do today: surfing, sailing, rafting, fishing, trekking, a four-wheel drive through the sand dunes or a horse ride along the beach? Where am I? Australia.

7 Few of the tourists who visit the beaches of southern Europe every year give any thought to their impact on the local environment. Yet they consume millions of litres of water, eat tonnes of fresh fruit and vegetables and produce huge volumes of waste.

8 Marjorie and her partner were both 40 when they got married. 'I discovered I was pregnant the day after our first anniversary,' says Marjorie. Her first child, Robbie, was born when she was 42. 'We were delighted.'

7 🔑 Work in pairs and discuss what techniques the writers have used in each of the eight opening paragraphs in activity 6 to try and hold readers' attention.

Emphasising

One of the article-writing techniques listed on page 34 was that it is more effective to express yourself forcibly or emphatically rather than in a flat way. You can, of course, do this by using interesting words and expressions, e.g. intensifying adverbs such as *enormously*, *truly*. But there are also some grammatical structures in English which you can use to lend emphasis to what you are saying. Using a less common word order can, for example, give extra emphasis to a sentence. So can adding an auxiliary verb to a statement – this must be stressed when speaking. (I *do* love you, for instance.) Adverbs and modal verbs can also be used for emphatic effect.

8 Look at the pairs of sentences below. In each case, which is the more emphatic? Why? Work with a partner and discuss your answers.

1 a) Mauritius is the most spectacular island I have ever visited.
   b) The most spectacular island I have ever visited is Mauritius.

2 a) Despite friends' warnings about the tedium of 25 hours in a cramped aeroplane, I actually enjoyed the flight to St Louis.
   b) Despite friends' warnings about the tedium of 25 hours in a cramped aeroplane, I did actually enjoy the flight to St Louis.

3 a) We spent a successful day deep-sea fishing.
   b) We spent an unexpectedly successful day deep-sea fishing.

4 a) Rarely have I been so impressed by a hotel's service.
   b) I have rarely been so impressed by a hotel's service.

5 a) I shall always remember our final evening's barbecue on the beach.
   b) What I shall always remember is our final evening's barbecue on the beach.

6 a) Mauritius must be one of the most romantic honeymoon spots in the world.
   b) Mauritius is one of the most romantic honeymoon spots in the world.

9 ⌐○ **Express each of these statements in two different and more emphatic ways, using the techniques illustrated in activity 8.**

1 Luigi's is the most exotic restaurant I have ever been to.
2 I enjoyed the disco despite its deafening music.
3 I have never before seen such a spectacular sunset.
4 We shall always remember the picturesque harbour.
5 We spent a memorable day climbing the highest mountain on the island.
6 James is one of the most intriguing people I have ever met.

10 ⌐○ **Complete the sentences below in any way that you wish. Then compare your sentences with those of other students in the class.**

1 Never have I been more afraid than ....
2 What I shall never forget is ....
3 The most exhilarating moment in my life was ....
4 I did enjoy ....
5 .... must be the most romantic place I have ever been to.

Avoiding dull words

Another important aspect of keeping readers' attention is to use interesting words and to avoid dull ones. One word which is best avoided in more formal writing is *get*. It is a word with so many possible meanings that it is better when writing to choose something with a more precise meaning e.g. *win, buy, persuade*. Moreover, it is more important stylistically to avoid repetition in more formal writing; a word like *get*, which is very useful in speaking or informal writing, will look strange if used too often in formal writing. Words like *nice, good, bad* and *terrible* are frequently used when someone is speaking or writing a letter to a friend. It is better to avoid them in more formal writing because, on the whole, they are very weak words which can suggest a range of meanings depending on the tastes of the speaker. It is usually possible to find a word which expresses a much more precise meaning and is, therefore, much more effective when your aim is to interest readers who do not know you and have very little idea what *nice* may mean in this context.

11 🔑 How many words can you think of to replace the underlined words in the sentences below? Some initial ideas are suggested for the first sentence. Notice how the other words suggested add an extra meaning that is not there with *nice*. Work with a partner and try to think of at least six words for each sentence. Then compare your words with those of other students in the class.

Example: *1 exhilarating, romantic, relaxing, memorable*

1 We had a <u>nice</u> week in Mauritius.
2 The island is <u>good</u>.
3 We had a <u>bad</u> time in the hotel.
4 They are very <u>nice</u> people.
5 The weather was <u>good</u> while we were there.
6 The hotel manager was <u>terrible</u>.

Planning articles

An article must be well structured with a beginning, a middle and an end. It must have distinct paragraphs with a clear topic in each one and the paragraphs should progress in a logical way. You need to plan what you are going to say before you start. For a CAE-type article of about 250 words, you probably need to think in terms of writing four or five paragraphs (including the introduction and conclusion).

Here is a possible plan for an answer to task 1 from the beginning of the unit. The question asked for an article for a college magazine about a proposed programme of social activities.

<u>Introductory question</u> – Did you find it difficult to find things to do last term?

<u>Paragraph 2</u> – reminder of last term's problems (few things to do, hard to meet other students etc.)

<u>Paragraph 3</u> – outline of programme (films, discussion groups, visiting speakers, excursions, discos), giving examples of each type of activity

<u>Paragraph 4</u> – advantages of the programme (cheap, maybe useful in studies, can meet other students from college etc.)

<u>Conclusion</u> – strong encouragement to attend (I'll certainly be there!)

12 🔑 Choose one of the other tasks from the beginning of the unit and write a plan for the article. Compare your plan with those of other students in the class.

Write the article you have planned. Try to use the tips and techniques from this unit as you write your answer.

Narratives

The aim of this unit is to answer the following questions.
- What kind of narrative might CAE ask you to write?
- What are the characteristics of good narratives?
- How can you think up effective content for a story?
- How can you tell a story in a particularly interesting way?
- How can you use more vivid verbs when telling a story?

In CAE Paper 2 you are unlikely to be asked to write something explicitly called a short story. You will not, for example, be asked to write a short story beginning 'It was a day I shall never forget ...' or one ending. 'We never saw each other again', as you perhaps were in FCE. However, many CAE questions do involve you in writing narrative in some form or another. You may, for example, be asked to write an article with a strong story element in it. It may be a letter or a report in which you have to recount some personal experiences; it may be a review in which you have to retell the plot of a film or book. It may take some other form. Do not be confused by the name which the task is given. If the task involves recounting an experience or telling a story in some way, then you will require narrative skills – although you may also, of course, need to use skills specifically relevant to writing letters, reports, articles or reviews as well.

This unit focuses on thinking about how you can write narrative in the most effective way, whether that narrative be framed in a letter, an article, a report or some other text type.

Here are four CAE-type tasks requiring you to write narratives.

1 You are the secretary of your local English club and you are expected to write an article for the newsletter in which you describe the meetings which have been held during the last three months. The club has had three meetings of very different types. One, in particular, was a great success. Write your article.

2 You have just been the witness of a crime. Fortunately, no-one was seriously hurt but there were some minor injuries and some valuable things were stolen. Moreover, some property was damaged. The police have asked you to write a full statement in which you describe exactly what you saw. Write your statement.

3 Last summer you spent a month working in another country. The agency which organised your job has asked you to write a report for the benefit of other people considering using the agency. You have been asked to focus on the most memorable experiences which you had and what you learnt from those experiences. Write the report.

4 Last week you saw a film whose story made a very strong impression on you. Write a review for your college newspaper in which you summarise the story of the film and explain why it affected you.

What makes a good story?

1 Can you think of any examples of stories or writers – in any language – that you like a lot or that you strongly dislike? Can you explain why you like or dislike them?

STUDY TIP

Remember that one of the best ways of improving your own written English is to read as much as possible. So, make a note of any good writers who are recommended and who you think that you might like to read. It is worth noting that many writers who did not write originally in English may well have been translated so that you can read their work in English too. You may find it particularly useful to read stories in English that you are already familiar with in your own language.

2 🔀 What are the characteristics of a good story? As a class, suggest everything that comes to mind. Note down on a separate piece of paper all your ideas. Then list the five or six most important characteristics for you personally.

3 🔀 The following texts tell much the same story but the second one is more effective than the other. Work with a partner and discuss what techniques have been used to make this version more effective.

1 About ten years ago, I was staying with some friends when they were burgled. We were on our way to bed when there was a knock at the door. Ron opened the door and saw two men on the doorstep asking for some water for their car. Ron brought them some but they didn't take it to the car, they threw it in his face and pushed past him into the house. They rushed round the house grabbing what they could, mainly some jewellery and a video recorder. They threw a television set through the glass patio doors and jumped after it, escaping through the back garden. It was over in seconds but it took us all some time to recover from the shock.

2　Some years ago, I was spending a few days with Anita, an old school
friend, her husband and her new baby. It was early January and there had
been an unusually heavy snowfall. My friends had just moved into a new
house on a secluded modern estate in Birmingham. Their home had a
large garden bordering on a park and the houses on either side were still
unoccupied; so we were really quite isolated from the world.

We had had a pleasant evening in the warm house feeling safe and
cocooned from the snow and the silence outside and were on our way to
bed. Suddenly, there was a knock at the door. Anita's husband, Ron, threw
on a dressing gown and went to answer it. 'Our car's broken down. Could
you possibly let us have a bucket of water for it?' asked one of the two men
standing there. Ron quickly filled a bucket for them and then shrieked as
they threw it over him and dashed past him. I was in the bathroom and
looked out to see two strangers rushing up the stairs towards me. I don't
suppose I've ever slammed a door so quickly. I leant hard against it
praying the lock was strong. I could hear Anita screaming 'Don't touch my
baby, don't touch my baby.' And then there was the noise of feet clattering
down the still uncarpeted stairs, a loud crash of breaking glass and
silence.

A few seconds later I heard Ron ringing the police and I cautiously
emerged from the bathroom. At the same time Anita came out of the
bedroom clutching the baby – who was still sound asleep. The men had
snatched the rings, ear-rings and watch which she had just taken off. They
had also grabbed the video recorder. The crash of broken glass was the
sound of the television being thrown through the patio doors. We could see
their footprints in the snow leading down the garden and away into the
park beyond.

We sat and shivered, both from the cold now streaming in through the
broken doors and from the shock, until long after the police had been and
taken our statements. I don't think any of us will ever feel quite so secure
in our own homes as we used to before that evening.

4 🔄 This activity focuses on some of the techniques which were used to make the second text in activity 3 more interesting. Compare the techniques below with those you discussed in activity 3. Did you think of all six? Then answer the questions about each of the techniques.

1 Variety of tenses
   a) Which is the most common tense to use when telling a story?
   b) When is it particularly appropriate to use the past progressive when telling a story?
   c) When is it particularly appropriate to use the past perfect when telling a story?
   d) What other tenses might occasionally be used when telling a story and in what circumstances?

2 Direct speech
   a) What examples of direct speech are there in the story?
   b) How could the same thing have been conveyed in indirect speech?
   c) What is the effect of using direct rather than indirect speech?

3 Vivid verbs
   a) Adjectives and adverbs are often used for descriptive purposes but verbs can also help to describe an action. By using an interesting or vivid verb the writer can give us a precise idea of how someone spoke or acted. Can you find any examples of such 'vivid verbs' in the story on the opposite page?

4 Description of setting
   a) What elements of the setting are described in the story on the opposite page?
   b) Why is it useful to describe these elements of the setting?
   c) Would it have been useful to describe the precise layout of the house or the furniture in the sitting-room?

5 Appeal to the five senses
   a) What are the five senses?
   b) How many of them are appealed to in the story on the opposite page?
   c) How might it have been possible to appeal to the other senses too?

6 Reference to feelings
   a) How many characters are there in the story?
   b) What do we know about the feelings of each of them?
   c) How do we know this?
   d) What else could the writer perhaps have said about the characters' feelings?
   e) How many ways can you think of in which a character's feelings can be conveyed to the reader in a story?

5 Below you have an example of a basic story which is not particularly well told. Work with a partner and discuss how you could use the six techniques listed in activity 4 – and any others you may have discussed in the unit so far – in order to tell the story more effectively. You may add any details that you wish to the story and can, indeed, change some of the elements if you feel it would make a better story. Then compare your ideas with those of other students in the class.

> One of the most exciting days of my life was my eleventh birth-day. It was a lovely sunny July day. I was on an island to the north of Scotland where, every summer, my father took a group of students on an archaeological dig on the site of a ruined medieval church. Suddenly one of the students called out in excitement. He had found something unusual. The group spent all day carefully unearthing a hoard of old silver bowls and brooches. Two days later I even had my name in the local newspaper.

The content of a story

EXAM TIP

The most difficult part of writing a narrative may be thinking of the idea for the story. Remember that:
YOU DON'T HAVE TO TELL THE TRUTH WHEN WRITING A STORY IN AN ENGLISH EXAM!

Although a writing task will often ask you to write about something that has happened to you, you can take any story and tell it in the first person as if it was your own personal experience. You could take a story:

- that has happened to a friend or relation of yours.
- that you've read in a magazine or newspaper.
- that is based on something you've seen on television.
- that is simply from your own imagination.

6 Look back at the first two CAE-type tasks at the beginning of the unit. Work with a partner and discuss how you could use each of the four sources listed above in order to get some basic ideas for your writing. Then compare your ideas with those of other students in the class.

7 Work with a partner and prepare a brief outline of a plot for a story based on two of the topics below. Write about 50 words. Then compare your ideas with those of other students in the class.

a) a disappointment in love
b) a disastrous holiday

c) the content of a song that is currently popular

d) a picture or notice on the classroom wall

Organising the story in an interesting way

Once you have decided on your story, it is important to organise the telling of it in an effective way. One step towards doing this is to begin the story in a way that will interest the reader.

8 ⌐o Look at the third task at the beginning of the unit. Work with two or three other students and decide whether the opening sentences suggested below are good ones or not – and why (not).

1 Very little that was memorable happened during my month in England as I spent most of my time at home looking after my hostess's two-year old twins while she went off to meet her friends in town.

2 From the moment I stepped onto the plane that would take me to Heathrow my month was to be memorable.

3 My very first day in England was the highlight of the whole time I was to spend there.

4 Nothing about England was to turn out as I had expected.

5 After filling in the agency's forms applying for work in England I had to wait a long time until any response came.

6 Last summer I spent a month in London working as an au pair for a family called Smith.

9 ⌐o Read the closing sentences from six stories. Note that two of them are endings which link up with two of the opening sentences from activity 8. Which of the following techniques have been used to end the stories?

– linking the ending to to the beginning in some way

– summing up the experience of the story in some way

– providing an unexpected surprise

1 This story may seem curious but I assure you that every word of it is true.

2 It was only then that I realised that I had come to the wrong house.

3 It was not until I eventually stepped off the plane that had taken me home that I was at last able to take a deep breath and relax.

4 It is only now, some weeks after these events occurred, that I can fully appreciate how John must have felt that day and I am truly sorry for the way I behaved.

5 On the flight home, relieved at last to be escaping from my loneliness, I discovered that my cousin had been staying in the next street.

6 Although I enjoyed my entire stay in England, nothing would ever quite equal the excitement of that first day.

Using vivid verbs

10 ☛ It is useful to have a repertoire of verbs which you can use instead of *say*. In the box below are some useful verbs. Make up some sentences which reflect the kind of speaking each verb describes.

Example: *'Moreover, it's too expensive,' he added.*

> add beg boast complain declare insist murmur order
> promise shriek snap stammer threaten warn whisper

Read out your sentences – but do not say the speaking verbs – and see how quickly other students can guess which verb you had in mind.

11 ☛ It is often possible to use more interesting verbs than *go*. How many can you think of? Write an appropriate sentence for each verb.

Example: *crawl – The traffic was so bad that the bus crawled along.*

12 ☛ Here are some other vivid verbs of different types. Match the subjects on the left with appropriate verbs in the middle and a phrase on the right to complete the image.

Example: *1 Rain patters on a metal roof.*

1 rain	giggle	an apple
2 tired cold people	screech	in the distance
3 thunder	patters	at a poor performance
4 heavy traffic	creaks	past on a motorway
5 car tyres	hisses	in a corner (to keep warm)
6 a dissatisfied audience	thunders	before speaking in public
7 an old door	munches	on a metal roof
8 children	huddle	on wet roads
9 a nervous person	trembles	at a joke
10 a hungry person	rumbles	on its hinges

Planning and writing

It is advisable to make a paragraph plan for a piece of narrative writing just as it is for any other writing task. A typical CAE-length story – 250 words – is likely to have four or five paragraphs. The first paragraph will often be used to set the scene, the second to third or fourth will tell the body of the story and the final paragraph will bring the story to an effective conclusion.

13 Choose one of the story outlines you discussed in activity 7 or one of the tasks from the beginning of the unit. Write notes indicating what each paragraph would contain. Then write a complete narrative, using the techniques we have discussed in the unit.

6 Reports

The aim of this unit is to answer the following questions.

- What kind of report might CAE ask you to write?
- What are the characteristics of an effective report?
- What style is appropriate when writing a report?
- How can you structure your paragraphs in the most appropriate way?
- How can linking words and expressions be effectively used?
- How can you present your ideas effectively?

Here are four CAE-type questions requiring you to write reports.

1 You recently took part in a one month exchange programme in which you attended a school / college in another country and lived with a local family while their son or daughter went to your school / college and lived with your family. You have now been asked to write a report for the organisers of the exchange programme commenting on different aspects of the programme. They have asked you to comment on travel, study and accommodation arrangements and to deal also with any language or cultural problems which arose. You should refer both to your own and to your exchange partner's experience.

2 The multi-national company which you work for has asked you to write a report on the current situation in your country. They want to know about a major economic or social problem that your country is facing at the moment, its nature and its causes and about what attempts are being made to solve it. They would like you to conclude by commenting on the extent to which this problem affects the company's work in your country.

3 You feel that your local community would benefit enormously from improved sporting or entertainment facilities and you have a particular project in mind. Write a report for your local council in which you describe your project, explaining why you feel it is necessary and what improvements it would bring.

4 You have been asked by someone doing research into language learning to write a report on your language-learning experiences so far. They would like you to describe which languages you have learnt and how you have learnt them. They would like you to say what you feel have been the strengths and weaknesses of the ways in which you have learnt the various languages that you know and to indicate how you intend to keep up your languages in the future.

The characteristic of a report

What exactly is a report? The dictionary defines a report as an 'official document that discusses something'. (*BBC English Dictionary*)

1 ☞ **What kind of document did each of these texts come from? How do you know?**

A

The Hotel de Paris

offers the kind of luxury that dreams are made of. The bedrooms are spacious and comfortable with every amenity you could wish for and the public rooms are stylish and gracious, redolent of a bygone age. A stay at the *Hotel de Paris* will provide any guest with some very special memories that will last a lifetime.

A spectacular Honeymoon Suite is available for those newly-wed couples who wish to start their new life in romantic splendour. Business Suites are also available for international business people who wish not only to stay at the *Hotel de Paris* but also to enjoy the hotel's comforts during their meetings too.

C

As soon as she entered the hotel, she felt as if she was in a different world. Perhaps after all the weekend would be a success. It all now depended on what kind of a mood John would be in when he arrived. If he arrived.

She decided not to register immediately but to order coffee in the lobby. She chose a deep leather arm-chair shielded by an enormous cheese-plant. While she could observe people coming into the hotel, no-one would be able to recognise her through its expansive foliage.

B

It's a lovely hotel right in the centre of town and the rooms are extremely comfortable. The only problem really is the traffic noise which doesn't let up much all night. Still, it's worth it to be in easy walking distance of the sights. And the shops!

Am thinking of you back in rainy old England. How are things at work now? Wish you could be here too!

D

Location
The Hotel de Paris is set in a side road off one of the main streets in the old historic centre of the town.

Accommodation
It has thirty double and ten single rooms all with en suite bathroom, colour satellite television and minibar. All the rooms are spacious and half of them face onto a relatively quiet central courtyard.

2 What characterises the report as a type of writing? Work with a partner and list as many characteristics as you can think of. Then compare your ideas with those of other students in the class. Add any other ideas to your list.

3 Compare the characteristics you noted in activity 2 with those in the list below.

- clear layout
- clearly differentiated paragraphs, often with headings
- clear introduction giving the basic facts
- neutral or formal language – vocabulary and structures
- content is usually presented objectively although it may then lead to a more personal conclusion

Paragraphs and headings

4 ☞ One of the most important characteristics of a well-written report is that it contains clearly differentiated paragraphs. Below you have some paragraph headings made by one student when planning the first two reports on page 47. Decide which paragraphs go with which report. Then number the paragraph headings in what seems to you to be the most logical order.

Accommodation arrangements   Action currently being taken
Causes of unemployment in Scotland today   Problems encountered
Economic and social effects of unemployment   The main problem
Implications of Scottish unemployment for X and Y Ltd
Introduction – basic details of own participation   Study arrangements
Introduction – the current situation in Scotland
Travel arrangements   Conclusion – recommendations

> **STUDY TIP**
>
> Always use paragraph headings to plan a report that you are writing. In some cases, you may decide to include your headings in your report; in other cases, they may simply remind you of the points you need to include. Before you begin writing, make sure that the headings are in the most logical order. As you write, make sure that everything that you include is in the most appropriate paragraph.

5 ☞ Work with a partner and prepare a plan for the last two reports on page 47. Make a list of paragraph headings in their most appropriate order. Then compare your plans with those of other students in the class.

6 🔑 Read the report below and suggest an overall title. Then suggest headings for each paragraph.

1 ....
Last month we sent a team of three members of staff to assess the town of Camford as a potential location for a new English language college for speakers of other languages. This report outlines the findings of the team and concludes with a recommendation.

2 ....
There are a number of basic geographical reasons why Camford would appear to be an attractive location for a language college. Firstly, it is situated at a distance of only fifty miles from London and there are good rail and bus connections with the capital. Secondly, although Camford is mainly known for its ancient university, it also has a number of other further education colleges so that there are substantial groups of young people in the city in term-times. Moreover, links between local industry, much of which is based on modern technology, and the educational institutions are growing so that the economy of the area is relatively healthy.

3 ....
The health of the local economy combined with the youthful nature of the population, inevitably has a positive effect on the facilities available in the town. These include a sports complex with, among other things, a skating rink and an Olympic-sized swimming pool, five cinemas, three theatres and two large concert halls. There are also numerous shops catering especially for the interests of the young.

4 ....
Despite its many fine points, Camford has, nevertheless, a couple of not insignificant disadvantages as the location for our new language school. First of all, there is a lack of appropriate rented accommodation available. In addition, public transport within the city is extremely poor.

5 ....
To conclude, our recommendation is that we should take our investigation of Camford as a suitable location a stage further and should look for an appropriate site within walking distance of the town centre. We should, however, also consider the possibility of providing residential accommodation for our students.

7 In any kind of writing it is important to structure your paragraphs well. Work with a partner and discuss these questions about paragraphing. Then compare your answers with those of other students in the class.

1 How do you make it clear where one paragraph ends and the next begins?
2 How many sentences would you expect to have in most paragraphs? (You will, of course, find lots of exceptions.)
3 In a CAE writing task of about 250 words, how many paragraphs would you expect to write?
4 What is the topic sentence of a paragraph?
5 What is the most usual place to find the topic sentence?

8 Look at the report in activity 6 and check whether the paragraphs in the report illustrate your answers to the questions in activity 7.

9 Work with a partner and look back at the paragraph headings you worked with in activity 5. Choose one of the reports you worked on in activity 5 and write a topic sentence for each of the paragraphs.

Linking words and expressions

STUDY TIP

Just as headings can clarify the structure of a piece of writing, so do linking words and expressions like for instance, firstly, besides, furthermore and as a consequence. It is, however, easy to overuse connecting words – or to use them wrongly. Practise using them accurately and appropriately and your work will be clearer to follow.

10 Look at the report in activity 6 again. Underline all the linking words and expressions. Then explain the function of each of the underlined words and expressions.

Example: *Firstly* – to introduce the first point.

11 ☞ **Answer these questions on connecting words and expressions.**

1 Suggest a synonym for *however* as in the sentence: *Camford, however, does have some disadvantages as a location.*
2 Can you think of two synonyms for *moreover*?
3 How could you say *to conclude* in another way?
4 If *firstly* and *secondly* can be used to introduce the first two points being made, what could be used to introduce the last point?
5 Explain the difference between *consequently* and *subsequently* and give a synonym for each.
6 Complete the blanks with one word.
   a) There are a number of reasons .... we make such a recommendation.
   b) That was the main reason .... his behaviour.
   c) Oxbridge, ... the contrary, is an ugly city.
   d) Oxbridge is, ... contrast, an ugly city.
   e) .... comparison .... Camford, it has little to recommend it.
   f) .... contrast .... Camford, it has little to recommend it.
   g) According .... historians, the town was founded in the 10th century.
   h) .... our opinion, Camford is a good choice.
   i) Camford is, ... the point of view of young people, an exciting place to be.
7 When might it be appropriate to say *last but not least*?

12 ☞ **Explain the difference between these pairs or groups of sentences.**

1 a) Firstly, I was impressed by the quality of the service provided.
   b) At first I was impressed by the quality of the service provided.

2 a) Lastly, it has a swimming pool and other sports facilities.
   b) At last, it has a swimming pool and other sports facilities.
   c) At least it has a swimming pool and other sports facilities.

3 a) From the supplier's point of view, the location is inconvenient.
   b) In the supplier's opinion, the location is inconvenient.

4 a) On the other hand, its spaciousness is very attractive.
   b) On the contrary, its spaciousness is very attractive.

5 a) Moreover, it is within easy reach of the capital.
   b) However, it is within easy reach of the capital.
   c) Therefore, it is within easy reach of the capital.

6 a) As far as we are concerned, the hotel would satisfy our requirements.
   b) What concerns us is whether the hotel would satisfy our requirements.

Presenting your ideas effectively

13 ⚡ Look at each of the pairs of texts below and decide which presents its ideas more effectively. Why?

1 a) The project was a great success. All the participants enjoyed it. It supplied some income for the company. It also provided a useful service for the community. It led to some good publicity for our organisation too.

   b) The project was a great success. Not only did all the participants enjoy it but it also provided a useful service for the community. As far as our company is concerned, it both supplied some income and led to some good publicity as well.

2 a) There were, however, one or two minor problems. Just over half of the participants expressed some dissatisfaction with the catering; the meals were too small and lacked variety. As many as sixty-five per cent of participants were unhappy with the accommodation provided, the main complaint being that they did not like having to share a room with two or three other people. We would strongly recommend that improvements be made with regard to both catering and accommodation in future years.

   b) There were, however, one or two minor problems. Many of the participants expressed some dissatisfaction with the catering and even more of them were unhappy with the accommodation provided. We would strongly recommend that improvements be made with regard to both these areas in future years.

3 a) Most of the participants were good at the tasks they had to do. Some were particularly good at dealing with people while others were better at administrative or technical tasks. It would be good if, in future, we could carry out some kind of pre-project assessment so that we get a good idea in advance of where individuals' strengths lie. This would help us to get the best use from the time available.

   b) Most of the participants were good at the tasks they were required to do. Some were particularly skilled at dealing with people while others excelled at administrative or technical tasks. It would be advantageous if, in future, we could carry out some kind of pre-project assessment so that we are aware in advance of where individuals' strengths lie. This would help us to make the most effective use of the time available.

≫→

4 a) To sum up, the project was a success and we would ~~recommend~~ recommend that our organisation should not hesitate to become involved in future projects of a similar nature.

b) To sum up the ~~proje~~ project was a ~~success~~ and ~~we~~ we would recommend that ~~are~~ our organisation should not hesitate to become involved in future projects ~~of~~ of a similar ~~nature~~ nature.

EXAM TIP

It is a waste of time in the exam to write out your answer in full and then to rewrite it. However, you are sure to need to make some corrections as you write your work. Remember that you may well lose marks if your work is messy and difficult to read. So make any alterations as neatly and clearly as you can.

14 Discuss with the class how to avoid making messy corrections like those of the student who wrote text 4 b) in the previous activity.

Planning and writing

15 Choose one of the tasks from the beginning of the unit and plan your answer. Write the answer to the task you have chosen. Try to use the tips and techniques from this unit as you write your answer.

7

Writing about work

The aim of this unit is to answer the following questions.
- What kind of work-related tasks might CAE ask you to write?
- What vocabulary do you need to talk about your work accurately?
- How do you make connections between different sections of your writing?
- How do you end a piece of writing in an effective way?

There is always one question in CAE Paper 2 Section B which relates in some way to using English for work and / or study purposes. Here are four CAE-type tasks which relate to work in some way.

1 Your workplace is advertising a number of posts, including one which you would like to apply for. It would mean a good promotion for you. Write an application for the position, stating what you are applying for, describing your experience and qualifications and explaining why you feel you are a good candidate for the job.

2 A colleague from abroad is planning to visit your workplace or college to see how a typical week there compares with a week in his or her own workplace / college. Write him or her a letter describing what programme you would recommend for the week. Explain why you feel some of the activities recommended would be of particular interest and use.

3 A company from abroad is interested in opening a fast food restaurant in the main street of your home town. You have been asked to prepare a report for them to help them decide whether to go ahead with the project or not. You are asked to comment on the suitability of the location from the point of view of potential market, existing competition, local availability of workers, transport for materials and customers. You should also draw attention to any other factors which you feel are relevant in the situation. Your report should conclude with a recommendation as to whether to open such an outlet or not. Write the report.

4 You have been asked to write an article for the magazine of the school which you attended when you were a teenager. The article is intended to give advice to young people interested in embarking on the same career as you. You are asked to comment on whether you would advise such a step now that you have some experience of work. The editor would also like you to give some advice – especially regarding training and how to succeed in the job generally – to anyone interested in such a career. Write the article requested.

EXAM TIP

It is usually not advisable to choose the work-related question unless you already have some experience of work. Students who can produce an answer based at least to some extent on their own experience of a working environment produce much better answers to this kind of question. This is not simply because people with work experience have a sounder knowledge of the vocabulary they need – although this may certainly help – it is more that it is easier for such people to select appropriate content for their writing and to organise it in a way that would be suitable for a real workplace.

STUDY TIP

Even if you think you are unlikely to choose the work-related question in the exam, the skills work practised in this unit will still be of benefit to you. The vocabulary exercises, although focusing on the vocabulary of work, deal with words that you are likely to come across both in the 'real world' and in other papers in CAE. The language focus work on making connections is applicable to any task whether it is related to work or not.

1 ☞ Analyse the tasks at the beginning of the unit according to the categories in the table below. The first one has been done for you as an example.

Task	Text type required	Content of task	Target reader	Style required
1	application letter	name of job; outline of experience and qualifications; reasons why suitable for job	manager	formal
2				
3				
4				

Vocabulary of work

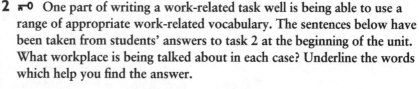

2 One part of writing a work-related task well is being able to use a range of appropriate work-related vocabulary. The sentences below have been taken from students' answers to task 2 at the beginning of the unit. What workplace is being talked about in each case? Underline the words which help you find the answer.

1 It'd be a good idea to spend some time in theatre helping pass over scalpels, swabs and the like. Of course, you'd have to scrub up first.

2 It might be interesting for you to attend a board meeting. You could even practise your English by taking the minutes if you'd like – if so, it'd help if you can do shorthand.

3 I'd recommend you spend at least a day in cosmetics. We have a very rapid turnover there and I think you'll understand why when you see what an impressive range we stock.

4 I've arranged a meeting with someone who can give you all the technical details you might need about the fertilisers we use on our crops. You'll be here just as we are gathering in the harvest and so you can see for yourself how our methods compare with yours.

5 All freshers should make an appointment to see their tutor this week. You are also recommended to visit Societies Fair in the Students' Union – open every day for the first week of term.

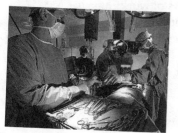

3 If you are already in work or have experience of work, write down five nouns, five verbs, five adjectives and five adverbs that you associate in some way with your workplace. If you have no work experience, write words connected with studying. Work with a partner and explain the associations your words have with your experience of work or study.

Making connections between different sections of your writing

In any piece of writing it is important to make connections between different parts of your writing – between sentences and between paragraphs. This helps the reader to follow your train of thought and makes your work much easier to read. You can make connections by using:

1 – conjunctions, e.g. *when, although, in case.*
2 – connecting adverbs or adverbial phrases, e.g. *nevertheless, in the end, generally speaking.*

It is important to have a good range of connecting words and phrases at your command so that you can use them effectively – as discussed in Unit 6, it is probably better not to use connectors at all than to use them inappropriately.

4 🔑 Look at the connecting words and phrases in the box and list them under the appropriate headings. They are all words used to join two parts of one sentence. Note that some of them may fit under more than one heading. Some have been done to start you off.

although	as	as if	as long as	as though	because
before	despite the fact that		even though	hardly	if
in case	in order not to		in order that	in order to	
just as	like	much as	provided	no sooner	since
so as to	so that	supposing	the moment	to	unless
until	when	whenever	whereas	while	whilst

Time	Condition	Purpose	Reason	Manner	Concession
as	as long as	in order not to	as	as	although

5 🔑 Choose the best connecting word or phrase from the box below to complete the following sentences.

as though	despite the fact that	hardly	in case
in order to	no sooner	provided	the moment

1 .... had Jane left college than offers of work came in.
2 .... Jack left college, he set off round the world.
3 .... had Mary left college when she realised she was expecting their first child.
4 The Director looked very pale at the meeting, ... he had just received some very bad news.
5 I have been promised a job as a trainee manager in my uncle's hotel, ... I pass all my final-year school examinations.
6 Her parents encouraged her to do a secretarial course .... she could not find work as an actress.
7 I had some coaching in maths before the exam .... increase my chances of passing.
8 John was not offered the job .... he was the best applicant.

6 🔑 Complete the sentences below in any logical way.

1 I became a politician in order to ....
2 He has detested his boss since ....
3 She enjoys her work although ....
4 James got a good job in a bank whereas ....
5 The new employee walked into the office as if ....
6 Jim has a coffee break whenever ....
7 I'll accept the job as long as ....
8 I wouldn't consider working for him – much as ....

7 🔑 The groups below contain connecting adverbials of a similar type. Work with a partner and discuss what heading you could give each group. Add at least one more word or expression to each group.

Example: 1 adding information – *besides, on top of that, too*

1 also, as well, at the same time, furthermore, moreover
2 again, equally, likewise
3 by contrast, however, instead, nevertheless, on the other hand, otherwise
4 accordingly, so, therefore, thus
5 in conclusion, to sum up
6 according to my mother, as I see it, in my opinion, personally
7 firstly, last but not least, next, secondly
8 afterwards, at first, subsequently, then
9 at last, eventually

8 🔑 Work with a partner. In each sentence below, one of the options does not have the same meaning as the others or it may not make logical sense. In each case, which option is the odd one out and why? Does it make sense in the context? If so, what meaning does it convey? If not, write a sentence or pair of sentences using the odd one out in a logical way.

1 Janet is a first-class nurse. ...... , her standards of hygiene at home leave something to be desired.
   A However   B Nevertheless   C Otherwise   D Nonetheless

2 .... , there are many reasons why Tolstoy is so highly considered as a novelist, despite any reservations one may have about his private life.
   A To conclude   B In conclusion   C All things considered

3 .... , he found a job.
   A Lastly   B At last   C Finally   D Eventually

4 .... , it would mean a deterioration in working conditions.
   A In my opinion   B As far as I am concerned   C To my mind
   D As I see it

5 Katie has a very good chance of getting the job. Michael, ... , is a very strong candidate.
   A likewise   B equally   C in the same way   D similarly

9 🔑 Which do you think is the more formal alternative in these pairs?

1 the conjunctions in activity 4
   a) *whilst, while*
   b) *to, so as to*
   c) *to, in order to / in order that*
   d) *no sooner, the moment*

2 the adverbials in activity 7
   a) *furthermore, moreover*
   b) *equally, again*
   c) *on the other hand, by contrast*
   d) *therefore, thus*
   e) *afterwards, subsequently*

10 🔊 Say where you would expect to find the adverbials listed with the sentences below – at the beginning, in the middle or at the end.

1 Salaries are good in the company. It has an excellent career structure.
also, as well, at the same time, besides, furthermore, moreover, on top of that, too

2 Valerie is an excellent typist. She is first-rate at shorthand.
again, equally, in the same way, likewise, similarly

3 We could promote Mary. We could promote her husband. She is very good at her job. Jim is not efficient at all. He is more popular.
alternatively, by contrast, however, instead, nevertheless, nonetheless, on the other hand

4 A: Mary is very good at her job.
B: She's very disorganised.
on the contrary

5 We must get started on the project. We won't finish the job on time.
otherwise

6 We were pleased with the company's work. We shall use them again.
accordingly, as a result, consequently, so, therefore, thus

7 The project was an unqualified success.
all things considered, in conclusion, to conclude, to sum up

8 The redundancies should never have been made.
according to my mother, as far as I am concerned, as I see it, in my opinion, personally, to my mind
Note that with *personally*, you need to change the original sentence.

9 Jim took over as manager when his uncle retired. He was his uncle's favourite nephew.
appropriately enough, broadly-speaking, certainly, chiefly, luckily, mainly, not surprisingly, primarily, significantly, surely, undoubtedly, unfortunately
Note that with *undoubtedly, chiefly, mainly* and *primarily* you need to join the sentences with a conjunction before adding the adverb.

10 The level of unemployment is an important factor in crime.
firstly, last but not least, lastly, next, secondly, thirdly

11 Jack jumped into the pool. Maria dived in.
afterwards, at first, beforehand, before long, immediately, subsequently, suddenly, then, within an hour

12 I waited for the bus. It arrived.
at last, eventually, finally

11 🔑 **Work with a partner. Have the underlined connecting words and expressions below been used correctly? If not, how could the texts be corrected? Compare your answers with those of other students in the class.**

1 I'll finish the sales report <u>while</u> I get home.
2 <u>Although</u> she has an important position in the company, she gets an excellent salary.
3 She decided to do a secretarial course <u>in case</u> she ever needed to find work in a hurry.
4 She worked very hard. <u>Therefore</u>, she got the sack.
5 I don't think we should offer him the job. <u>Firstly</u>, he has no experience. <u>Secondly</u>, he has no qualifications. <u>And, besides</u>, I don't like his manner.
6 Jane graduated from university with a first class honours degree in Spanish. Jill, <u>conversely</u>, has very good qualifications.
7 <u>As far as the management is concerned</u>, he is the perfect employee. His colleagues, <u>moreover</u>, know that he is extremely lazy.
8 She did very well at the interview and was, <u>subsequently</u>, offered the position <u>provided that</u> she agreed to do a typing course one evening a week.

12 🔑 **Now choose appropriate connectors from the lists in activity 10 to fill the gaps in the text. Do not use the same connecting expression more than once.**

The day started badly. (1) ...., Bill forgot to set his alarm clock and was, (2) ...., late for work. (3) ...., his boss told him that the report it had taken him two days to write was not satisfactory and would, (4) ...., have to be redone. (5) ...., he would have to get it done before leaving work that afternoon as it was needed for an important meeting the next morning. (6) ...., his girlfriend rang to say she did not want to go out with him any more. When Bill (7) .... got home, he decided it would be best to go to bed at once before any other disasters happened. (8) ...., it was not the end of his troubles for the day as he had no sooner fallen asleep than the telephone started ringing. Just as he reached it, it stopped. (9) ...., the next day was better altogether.

Ending a piece of writing in an effective way

It is important to end your writing in an effective way so that the reader is not left with a poor impression of your work. A good conclusion should do the following.

- It should sum up or round off what has gone before in some way.
- It should be in correct English.
- It should leave the reader with a positive final impression of the writer's work.

13 ▪O Here are the ways in which some students ended task 3 on page 55. Work with a partner and decide if it was an effective way of ending a writing task. Why (not)? Note that in some cases the weaknesses are to do with content whereas others are to do with accuracy.

1 It is impossible for me to say what you should do. That is for you as managers to decide.
2 I'm afraid I don't have any time to finish this report and so I cannot say more.
3 I would suggest to open a Chips Palace in Cae-on-Sea because of the reasons I did above.
4 I found this a rather boring subject and I am afraid I cannot think of anything else to write about it.
5 In conclusion, I would advise you to postpone making a decision until the city council elections are over in June.
6 So, it's over to you lot now for the pretty awful task of coming to a decision.
7 To sum up, I have no hesitation in recommending that you proceed with plans to open a Chips Palace in Cae-on-Sea.
8 Eventually, all things considering, I think you should to go ahead with the project. Otherwise, you could miss out on a golden possibility.

14 Write an ending for each of the other three work-related tasks from the beginning of the unit. Compare your endings with those of other students in the class and choose the ones you like the best.

8

Notes, notices and announcements

The aim of this unit is to answer the following questions.

- What kind of notes, notices and announcements might CAE ask you to write?
- What are the characteristics of this kind of writing?
- How can you express yourself briefly, clearly and precisely?
- What abbreviations are commonly used in this kind of writing?
- How can you avoid the most common spelling and punctuation errors?
- How can you help yourself to avoid making mistakes with words that are frequently confused?

CAE Paper 2 is most likely to ask you to write a note, notice or announcement in Section A because, in general, these are likely to be quite short pieces of writing and so are most appropriate as one part of a multi-part task. However, they may sometimes be elaborated somewhat and included in Section B.

Here are five CAE-type tasks requiring you to write notes, notices or announcements of different types.

1 You have just returned from spending some time with some friends in the USA. Write them a note to let them know you have arrived home safely and to thank them for their hospitality. Also tell them about some things which you forgot to bring home with you and let them know what you would like them to do with them. Write about 75 words.

2 You have made a provisional booking for your boss in a London hotel. She had a number of special requests for the hotel regarding her accommodation. The hotel is able to meet most of them but there is a problem with one particular request. Leave a note for your boss, explaining the situation and asking whether you should confirm the booking. Write about 70 words.

3 Some friends are going to spend a weekend in your flat while you are away. It is their first time in your country. Write them a set of notes in which you suggest how they should spend the weekend. Draw their attention to some interesting events and explain what to do if they'd like to go to them. Also ask them to do a couple of things for you while they are in the flat. Write about 250 words.

4 You have something which you would like to sell. Write a notice for your college notice board. Write about 50 words.

5 There are going to be some major changes at your college / workplace. These involve both staffing and the organisation of activities. Write an announcement for the college / workplace newsletter in which you provide clear information about the changes and how they may affect colleagues. Write about 250 words.

What are the characteristics of notes, notices and announcements?

1 ⚲ What are the main characteristics of notes, notices and announcements such as those in the five exam tasks? Look at the characteristics below and decide which three are particularly appropriate to the writing of notes, notices and announcements.

eloquence   creativity   brevity   originality   clarity
sophistication   precision   complexity   humour

2 ⚲ The following extracts have been taken from some students' answers to the five CAE-type tasks at the beginning of the unit. In each case there is a problem because the writer has not been either brief, clear or precise enough. Look at the answers and decide what the problem is in each case.

1 ... I think I left some things behind either in my room or in the bathroom. I'm really sorry but could you send them on to me, at my college address? I'll send you the money for the postage as soon as possible ...

2 Ms Head,

   I've made a provisional booking for you with a hotel in central London. They can provide the business and other facilities that you requested. However, there is one problem, which is a bit of a nuisance really. I wasn't sure whether I should go ahead with the booking or not but at least they took it on a provisional basis. Unfortunately, they've only got a room free for three days not the four that you wanted. Perhaps we could change your flights? Or should I try for a different hotel? Let me know what I should do.
   Jo

3 ... You could go to a concert at the Corn Exchange on Saturday. I think Madonna is going to be on or is it Michael Jackson? Mind you, it's probably too late to get hold of tickets now. I suppose I should have ordered some for you months ago. But then, of course, I didn't know you were coming months ago, did I? So perhaps you'd be better off going to the theatre. I'm not sure what's on but you can find out by ringing 334412 or is it 344214? Check in the phone book which you'll find beside the bedroom phone ...

4 The college library is going to be extended next month by Briggs and Co. There will be some disruptions while the work in being carried out. The south wing of the library will be closed for the first two weeks of the month and the north wing for the second two weeks. The catalogue rooms will be open all the time except the first two days of work. The central block will be most inconvenienced as it will be only partially open for the whole month with different sections open each week. You can get more precise information on exactly which bits will be open when from the Chief Librarian's Office. The library apologises for any inconvenience caused but assures readers that future services will be enormously enhanced by the extension.

5 **BOOKS FOR SALE.**
   Good quality.
   Ring Anne any time
   after 9.30.

3 🔑 The people who wrote the answers in activity 2 need some advice about writing notes, notices and announcements. Do you agree with the advice given below?

- You can present your message more clearly by laying the page out in a well-spaced way.
- It is usually not appropriate to write in one continuous paragraph.
- Remember to include precise details, e.g. dates, places.
- Present your information in a logical order.
- Do not include unnecessary detail.

4 🔑 Work with a partner and discuss what information must be included in each of the following tasks, e.g. *name of film*. Then work individually and write one of the three tasks. Do not write more than 50 words.

1 An announcement about a film which is to be shown in your school one evening.
2 A notice saying you are going on a long trip in your car and asking if anyone would like to come with you and share expenses.
3 A note to a friend saying that you are no longer able to do something together that you had arranged previously.

Abbreviations

> **TIP**
>
> The use of abbreviations is very common in notes; it helps with brevity and is appropriately informal. Remember, however, not to use too many abbreviations in your work, particularly in an exam.

5 🔑 Look at the notes and notices below. What abbreviations have been used and what do they stand for?

1
> *Off to London now.*
> *Home Thurs. Pls*
> *ring dr. asap.*

2
> **FOR SALE**
> Nearly new boy's
> bike, 28".
> £50 ono.

3
> **TO SHARE**
> Furn. flat, 2 bedrms, 2
> recep. rms, k. and b.,
> cent. htg. Central sit. Suit
> prof. m. or w. Rent –
> £250 pcm.

4
> VIP's eta. 16.00 hrs.
> Mtg with hd. of dept.
> till 16.30. Then dep.
> for HQ.

5
> *Do come to Jo's PARTY*
> *at 21 Sloane Tce*
> *Wed. 23rd Oct. 8 till late.*
> *RSVP   BYOB*

6
> *You can find the info.*
> *about JFK on pp. 338–9,*
> *3rd vol. of encycl. If you*
> *have probs., ask lib. asst.*

Punctuation and spelling

6 ▪○ **How does punctuation affect the meaning in the sentences below?**

1 a) She was very upset when she found out what her friend had been saying.
   b) She was very upset when she found out what her 'friend' had been saying.

2 a) My brother who lives in London is a zoologist.
   b) My brother, who lives in London, is a zoologist.

3 a) They're coming to the party together!
   b) They're coming to the party together?

4 a) We can't keep all the cats' kittens.
   b) We can't keep all the cat's kittens.

5 a) Some people say that regular cold baths are a good thing.
   b) Some people say that regular cold baths are a Good Thing.

6 a) Drop bombs. If attacked, then return to base without delay.
   b) Drop bombs if attacked. Then return to base without delay.

7 a) Were really excited to hear your news.
   b) We're really excited to hear you're news.

8 a) What did you think of Sam's wife?
   b) What did you think of 'Sam's Wife'?

7 🔑 The note and the announcement below have been written without punctuation. Read them and add all the capital letters and punctuation marks that are needed for them to make sense. You will also need to lay out the writing in a more appropriate way than one continuous paragraph.

A id love to go out with you and sally on tues night lets meet in the red lion on bridge st at 8 and then go if we can get tickets to the concert in the town hall the rocky horrors are playing have you heard of them i hadnt until a couple of weeks ago when jane took me to her cousins house and he was raving about them theyre a new english group apparently theyre really popular abroad already especially with french and japanese kids they had a smash hit in the states with lets tango in paris which almost got into the top ten here too its pretty good if you dont object to a heavy metal beat anyhow we can hear for ourselves next week if you agree ill give you a ring on sun to see what you think love harriet

B arts cinema cambridge mon 27 and tue 28 dec singing ringing tree a beautiful and haughty princess is tamed by a beast and a magic tree a rare treat for all those thirtysomethings who saw this east german classic on the television in the 60s it will charm the new generation too

STUDY TIP

Spelling

Spelling is important in all writing tasks. If you don't spell correctly, then your writing does not create a very good impression. Remember that English spelling is difficult because it often does not match pronunciation. Make a list of the words which you misspell most often. Work hard at learning how to spell these words correctly. You could even ask your friends to test you.

8 ⚷ In the text below there are thirty words which are frequently misspelt in English. In each case part of the word is written for you. Complete the words using the correct spelling.

I'm (1) wr..........ing to tell you about a (2) for ....n (3) prof..........or who visited our department on (4) We..........day. He gave a lecture on (5) gov..........ent funding of (6) sc..........ce, (7) espe..........ly (8) med..........ne and (9) ps..........atry. He was very interesting although at times his (10) pron..........ation made him (11) dif..........lt to follow. In general, however, his use of the (12) lang..........ge was very (13) skil..........l. He (14) ref..........red to some (15) fa..........ating (16) res..........ch being done in (17) Br..........il at the moment. He (18) rec..........nded that we tried to attend a conference in Rio in (19) Feb..........y and gave us the (20) ad..........ss of the (21) sec..........ry of the conference (22) com..........ee to write to for an (23) ap..........tion form. He suggested that I (24) of..........red to give a paper there on the (25) arg..........ents about the (26) rel..........nce of work done by contemporary (27) sc..........tists but I think I'd be too (28) emb..........sed. Perhaps we could consider giving a paper (29) tog..........r instead of two (30) sep..........ate ones?

Commonly confused words

Part of writing clearly is using the correct word. There are a number of words in English which can be easily confused.

9 Work with a partner and discuss the differences between the words in the groups. Then write sentences which clearly illustrate those differences.

advice / advise   practice / practise   assure / ensure / insure
chance / chances / possibility / opportunity   childish / childlike
died / dead   experience / experiment
hard / hardly   interested / interesting / bored / boring
lay (laid) / lie (lay) / lie (lied)   loose / lose
raise / rise / rouse / arouse   sensible / sensitive
used to / be used to / get used to   wear / carry / use

10 🔑 Choose one of the words from activity 9 to complete each of the gaps in the notices from a school notice board below.

1
Meeting 8 p.m. tonight
To discuss how to
.... money to build
a new gym
for the school.
Please come with as many
ideas as you can think of.

3
Do you want to
.... weight? Or
just to become a bit
fitter?
   Now's your
.... Come along
to tonight's aerobics
session in the school hall.

5
Don't .... in
bed until you're late
for school.
FOR SALE: reliable
alarm clock. Only £6.
Contact, Debbie,
class R2

2
Tonight At 7.30,
Sports Hall
FOOTBALL ....
All team members and
reserves should attend.

4
DEBATE TONIGHT
MOTION: All pupils
should have to
.... school
uniform.
   Come and listen,
join in the discussion
from the floor and
then cast your vote.

6
Class Y3 is carrying out
some .... into
telepathy. Have you ever
had any telepathic
...................? If so, you
might be a suitable subject
for our research. Please
contact Miss Homes if you
are .... in
helping us.

11 Work with a partner. Make up some notices with missing words like those in activity 10 and write each notice on a separate piece of paper. Display your notices around the classroom and give each notice a number (for identification purposes). Read the notices with your partner. Make a list of the missing words.

Planning and writing

12 Choose one of the first three tasks from the beginning of the unit and write a draft.

Exchange your work with another student. Look at each other's work critically. Is what has been written totally clear? Where does the language need correcting before a final draft is written? (Think about spelling, punctuation and choice of words as well as grammar.)

Underline anything that you feel should either be clarified or corrected. Discuss your underlined words with your partner. Rewrite your work in the light of your partner's comments.

Instructions and directions

The aim of this unit is to answer the following questions.
- What kind of instructions might CAE ask you to write?
- What are the characteristics of well-written instructions and directions?
- How can you make sure that your instructions or directions are clear?
- How can you choose the most appropriate word?
- How can you vary your sentence structure in an appropriate way?

Here are four CAE-type tasks requiring you to write instructions and directions. For each of the tasks you are expected to write about 250 words.

1 Some friends are going to stay in your flat while you are on holiday. They are keen walkers and have asked you to leave written directions of a walk in the area in the evening which will show them some interesting places. The walk, ideally, should take about two hours. Write them a note leaving clear directions and describing what they will see as they walk. Include some explanation as to why you chose the route you did.

2 You have lent a piece of valuable equipment to a friend for a month – a camera, a computer or a tape recorder, perhaps. Your friend has never used a piece of equipment like this before. Write him or her detailed instructions explaining how to use the equipment. Describe one or two problems that you have had with it and explain how you solved these problems. Also explain how they should look after the equipment so that it is returned to you in perfect condition.

3 Some friends from England are going to be staying in your home while you are away. They are very fond of playing games. You have lost the instructions of a favourite board game of yours, one that you think your friends may not know. Write out instructions in English for your friends so that they will be able to play this game.

4 You have an American friend who is a school-teacher. She is organising a party for her class of twenty eight-year-old children and she would like to make it a party typical of one for children from your country. She has written to you asking about how such parties are organised in your country. She is particularly interested in what kinds of games are played and what sort of food is served. She has also asked you about any party traditions typical of particular times of the year. You may include any other information that you think may be useful. Write her a letter, with the instructions she has requested, making sure that they are clear enough for her to organise a successful party.

The characteristics of well-written instructions

1 ⌐**0** Here are some instructions in answer to exam task 3. What is wrong with them?

> Snakes and Ladders is a really good game to play with the children. You'll find the board in the top drawer. To play it each person chooses a different coloured counter and places it on square number one. You take it in turns to throw the dice and move the number of squares indicated. If you land at the bottom of a ladder you move your counter up to the top of the ladder. You have to get a six before you can start playing. What you have to try and avoid is to land at the head end of a snake. Whenever you throw a six you get another turn. The first person to get to the beginning is the winner.

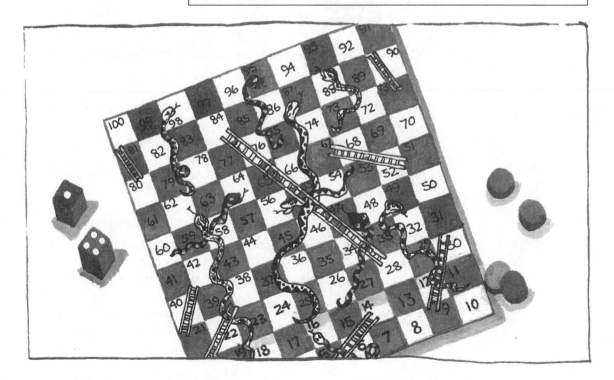

Making sure your instructions are clear

2 ☛ Read these instructions about how to do a magic trick. Put them in the most logical order.

Orange to Apple

a) As you remove the handkerchief, secretly take the orange peel with it.

b) Cover the 'orange' with it.

c) Crumple the handkerchief and put it, with the concealed orange peel, in your pocket.

d) Display a large handkerchief to show that it does not conceal anything.

e) Find a small apple and put the orange peel around it, so that it is completely hidden.

f) Hey presto, the orange has turned into an apple.

g) If they are not too close, they will not spot the slices in the skin.

h) Prepare an orange beforehand by peeling it carefully.

i) Set the 'orange' on a table in front of your audience.

j) Use four upward slices through the skin, leaving it joined at the top.

k) Then announce that you are going to remove the handkerchief and some magic will have happened.

3 ⏻ **Read these instructions about water-skiing and answer the questions.**

1 Does each paragraph have a distinct purpose? Make up a heading for each paragraph.
2 Look at the three underlined phrases. In what way does each of them play a part in making the instructions clearer?
3 Can you find any other examples of the following types of information, which all help make instructions clear?

– precise times and measurements
– precise verbs
– precisely defined objects
– reasons for doing something

Water-skiing

A water-skier is towed at speed behind a motor-boat, so before you start skiing make sure you know the safety signals between the tow-boat, look-out and skier. You should be a good swimmer.

You will need a wet suit for early summer and winter water-skiing and an approved water-ski safety jacket. Your tow-boat should be able to maintain at least 48 kph. Use an approved tow-rope <u>23 metres long</u>. Except in authorised competitions, water-skiing is not allowed at night – between one hour after sunset and one hour before sunrise.

Water skis are <u>made of laminated wood or fibre glass</u>, in varying lengths for children and adults. The average adult length is 1,700 mm. There are several types of ski for different skiing techniques but for beginners general purpose skis are best.

Practise on shore by wetting your feet and the foot bindings on the skis. Holding down the heel rubbers, slip your feet into the toe rubbers. Pull up the heel rubbers (adjusting the heel slide if your bindings are adjustable).

With your feet flat and set shoulder-width apart, <u>crouch on your skis with your knees drawn up to your chest</u>. Extend your arms forward outside your knees.

Hold the tow-bar while someone draws the tow-rope gradually taut. Keeping your feet flat, knees bent, arms and back straight and head up, let the rope pull you upright. Practise until you have mastered this movement.

When you are ready to move into water, start in waist-deep water, letting your safety jacket support you. Grasp the tow-bar, crouch as you did when practising on shore and keep your ski tips slightly above water in line with the stern of the boat.

As the boat idles forward and the rope draws tight, you will begin to move. When the rope is taut, signal to the driver of the tow-boat that you are ready and he or she will accelerate gradually. Hold your crouch position until the skis rise to the surface of the water and begin to plane, then straighten up slowly.

To stop, signal to the driver, then release the tow-rope and allow yourself to sink into the water, supported by your safety jacket.

4 ⏻ **How might each of the following instructions be made more precise?**

1 Leave the marinated meat to soak for some time.
2 Cut a triangle out of a piece of paper.
3 Regularly top up the anti-freeze.
4 Cut the vegetables before cooking.
5 Begin the exercise routine by lying on the floor.

5 🔑 Read the instructions for people who have difficulty sleeping. Work with a partner and correct any instructions which are incorrect.

- Take a stimulant – a cup of coffee, for example – before going to bed.
- Have a substantial meal not too long before you go to bed.
- Don't watch exciting films or occupy yourself with work problems in the evenings.
- Exercise in the morning rather than the afternoon or evening.
- Don't worry about not sleeping – that only makes matters worse.
- Warm milk at bedtime stimulates your digestive system and delays sleep.
- A soft mattress can help to encourage sleep.
- You can help yourself to relax after turning out the light by reciting poetry or imagining yourself in a favourite place.
- Close your eyes and imagine a line of polar bears. Counting them will help you to fall asleep.

Choosing the most appropriate word

English has a very large vocabulary. It often has five or six words which might all be translated by the same one word in another language yet it is important to use the right word in a particular context.

6 🔑 Look at the sentences below and choose the best word.

1 To play tennis you need a .... and a set of balls.
   A bat   B racquet   C club   D cue

2 To start a game of tennis, one player takes the ball and .... to his or her opponent.
   A hits   B scores   C serves   D heads

3 You lose the point if you hit the ball out of the .... without it bouncing.
   A court   B pitch   C field   D track

4 If it is not clear whether the ball was in or out, the ruling is made by the ....
   A judge   B referee   C umpire   D adjudicator

5 In a game of chess, the players take turns to move their ....
   A people   B bits   C counters   D pieces

6 The queen in chess can .... in any direction.
   A walk   B run   C go   D move

7 White always plays first in chess and it is customary to change colours with your .... after each game.
   A enemy   B rival   C opponent   D competitor

8 The aim of chess is to .... the other player's king.
   A capture   B catch   C arrest   D hunt

7 Choose your own favourite hobby – a sport, a game or a craft, perhaps. Make a list of all the words you can think of connected with that hobby. Ask your teacher or use a dictionary or an encyclopaedia to help you if necessary. Remember to think of verbs as well as nouns.

Read out your list to the other students in the class. They must guess which hobby you had in mind. They should also try to add some words to your list.

Varying sentence structure

8 🔑 Work with a partner and decide what activities the instructions below refer to.

1 Insert your card in the machine. Press the numbers corresponding to your personal identification number.
2 When you are introduced to someone it is polite to stand up, if you are sitting, and to shake hands.
3 You can use bottled or squeezed lemon juice or the juice from a grated onion. Dip a toothpick into the juice and write on hard-surfaced paper.
4 Move all your pots into a cool room where they will be away from direct sunlight.
5 Whisk two egg whites in a bowl until stiff. Add 50 g. of caster sugar and continue whisking until the mixture will stand in soft peaks and keep its shape.

9 🔊 Work with the same partner and write the instructions in activity 8 in a different way. Try to vary your sentence structure.

Example: 1 *Having inserted your card in the machine, press the numbers corresponding to your personal identification number.*

or

After inserting your card in the machine, you should press the numbers corresponding to your personal identification number.

10 🔊 What is wrong with this set of directions? Are they clear? Are they well expressed?

Come out of the station. Go straight ahead. You will come to a war memorial. Turn right. Cross the road at the zebra crossing. Take the third turning on the left. That is Bateman Street. The school is near the crossing. It is on the left and side of the station. You can't miss The school is ten minutes walk from the station.

[handwritten: David My class 4 2 Twe]

11 On a piece of paper, write a subject that you would like to receive instructions about. For example, how to make a good cup of coffee or how to make an omelette.

Exchange papers with a partner. Write instructions for the topic you were given. Make sure that you use a range of sentence structures. When you have finished, give your instructions to the student who requested them. Read each other's instructions carefully and, if necessary, ask each other questions to clarify anything that is not absolutely clear in the instructions. For example, *What exactly do you mean by 'after a little while'?* Then improve your instructions in accordance with your partner's questions.

Planning and writing

12 Choose one of the tasks from the beginning of the unit and plan your answer. Write the answer to the task you have chosen. Try to use the tips and techniques from this unit as you write your answer.

10

Reviews

The aim of this unit is to answer the following questions.
- What kind of reviews might CAE ask you to write?
- What are the characteristics of a good review?
- How can you make your style interesting and effective?
- How can you present your opinion convincingly?
- What words are useful for conveying positive and negative views?

Here are four CAE-type tasks requiring you to write reviews.

1 You have recently seen the film of a book which you had previously read. Write a review for your college magazine in which you compare the two, describing how closely you feel the film reflected the book and explaining which of the two you preferred and why.

2 An international magazine for young people is running a series of articles called 'Books which have influenced my life'. Each week someone describes one or more books which had an effect on their life, explaining how and why they were affected. You decide to write an article for the series.

3 You see this notice in a local English language magazine.

> *Join our team of reporters.* We are keen to recruit new writers for our team of sports reporters. Show us your skills by writing a 250-word review of two sporting events which you have recently seen. One of these should have made a positive impression on you while the other should have had a negative effect on you. If we are impressed by your work, we will publish it and will invite you to make further contributions to our columns. No payment but free tickets to a wide range of events.

Write the review.

4 You recently attended a music, film or drama two-day festival which is held annually. As a number of your colleagues share your enthusiasm for this particular branch of the arts you decide to write a review of the festival for your workplace magazine. In general, you enjoyed the festival very much although there were one or two disappointments. You should describe the festival as vividly as possible and should aim to attract other colleagues to attend it in future years.

The characteristics of a good review

1 ⚏ **Work with a partner and discuss these questions. Then compare your answers with those of other students in the class.**

1 What sorts of things are reviews written about?
2 Do you ever read reviews? If so, about what sorts of things?
3 How many of the following things should a review provide?
    a) basic information about the content of what is being reviewed –
       both what it is about and also practical details like where to see it,
       who produced it etc.
    b) the reviewer's personal opinion of the work
    c) a recommendation as to whether the readers of the review would or
       would not enjoy the book / film / music / video game / television
       programme being reviewed
    d) some helpful comments for the benefit of the performers / writers
       etc. involved in the work being reviewed
    e) an enjoyable piece of writing, with perhaps some relevance to
       aspects of life beyond the limits of the work under review

2 ⚏ **Read the review of a new series of television programmes on the opposite page. As you read, think about whether the reviewer is meeting the aims in activity 1. Then answer the questions below.**

1 What, in brief, is the subject of the review? List all the facts that are
   given in the review about the contents of the programme as well as
   any practical details about its production.
2 What is the reviewer's personal opinion of the programmes? Underline
   all the words and expressions which serve to express this.
3 Does the reviewer recommend that viewers watch or do not watch this
   series? How does she express this?
4 Would (a) the children and (b) the adults involved in producing these
   programmes feel that they had been given some useful comments in
   the review? If so, what?
5 Will readers enjoy reading this review? Is it of any interest when you
   have little chance of seeing the programmes described? Does the writer
   say anything that relates to a broader subject than the programmes
   reviewed? If so, what?

Children's Programmes a Hit

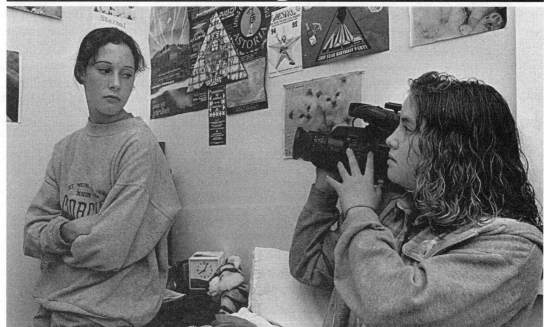

When it comes to explaining the shortcomings of the fatherless family, Kerry Dunn, aged 12, carries a lot more power, conviction and dignity than any politician has yet. Her short, home-made video, 'Life Without Dad', is the startling highspot of BBC2's new series of films, *As Seen on TV*. Kerry is angry, hurt, persistent in her questioning of what has happened to her and – herein lies the dignity – rather than being interviewed by some soapily compassionate reporter, she has made her own pitch.

It was about time that children, the most vulnerable and absorbed of television audiences, were invited to take over the means of production. The camcorder is now ubiquitous: the youngest children are television-literate, with most seven-year-olds perfectly capable of aping[1] a vox pop[2], a walking shot or a commentary.

Yet, so far, while adults make video diaries[3], all children have been invited to contribute to their generation's medium are silly clips[4] for the likes of Jeremy Beadle[5]. Eric Rowan and Chris Morris, of children's BBC, wanted to give children what Morris calls a 'chance to tell their own truth', and

have quartered[6] the country looking for willing film-makers, lending them camcorders and waiting for the tapes to arrive in the post.

Smaller children have at times been chaperoned, particularly for street interviews, but otherwise the material is in their hands. They interview their families, talk alone in their bedrooms to tripod cameras, a blind boy demonstrates how he sees the world, some surfers put their point of view in Scotland, an orphan in Brighton talks about living with grandparents, and in one of the more violent films, later in the series, two 12-year-old girls make a no-holds-barred[7] documentary on the horrors of having to share a bedroom. They were, apparently, shocked to see themselves.

Chris Morris edits the tapes, sends a rough-cut for approval by the child, tidies it up, and puts it out. The results are uneven, sometimes funny, sometimes passionate or silly. But they belong to the children and for once nobody is patronising them. Watching, other children may grasp the all-important fact that television is nothing magical, just another medium for communication.

---

1   copying
2   recording, often done by asking ordinary people on the street their opinions on some subject
3   a personal account of one's everyday life recorded by the subject using a video camera, a kind of diary on film
4   a short extract from a film
5   host of a TV show which shows home videos of people doing silly things
6   searched
7   totally frank

Writing with style

It is, of course, possible to write a review in a very straightforward way. The reviewer of *Children's Programmes a Hit* could, for example, have written something along the following lines.

> A new series of videos made by children is to start soon. It is certainly time that children were encouraged to make their own films. What they have produced is a series that is sometimes very powerful …

STUDY TIP

Writing with style is something that is extremely personal. It involves using your own experience and your own language skills to write in a particularly individual way. The best way to improve your writing style – in English, as in any language – is probably to read as widely as possible and then to experiment with your writing. The examination room is not the best place for experiment, of course, but it is a good idea to take advantage of the writing classes you have before the exam in order to try out some experiments with language on your teacher and your fellow-students.

3 🖘 Look at the following short extracts from a number of different reviews. 'Translate' each into straightforward English as in the paraphrase of the review *Children's Programmes a Hit* above. What techniques has the writer used to make his or her work more interesting than the paraphrase?

1 Teenagers are one of the few species so far not to have been made the subject of a nature programme. This is a pity. The greater spotted variety, legendary for its long periods of indolence interspersed with frantic spells of alien activity, fascinates naturalists and anthropologists alike.

2 Society: is it a free association, a living organism or an open prison? Or does it, as the Great Leaderene* wanted us to believe, not really exist, being only an accidental gathering together of free-floating and fiercely competing units, families, individuals? John Arden's *Live Like Pigs* (Theatre Upstairs) was written in 1958 but it could have been written last week …

* humorous nickname used to refer to Margaret Thatcher when she was Prime Minister

3

Whitney Houston is the Arnold Schwarzenegger* of soul. Other vocalists may exude more character, more sexiness, more charm even but for the sheer dimension and technical range of her voice, nobody else can touch her. In so far as a singer can be said to ripple and bulge with vocal muscles, she does.

* muscular, physically tough film star who played the lead in, for example, the Terminator films

4 ↗ When experimenting with style, native speakers also have to avoid a number of common stylistic errors. Can you identify what the stylistic errors are in the following sentences? Note that one or two of the examples are clumsy rather than strictly wrong.

1 The moment he opened his mouth, he realised he had put his foot in it.
2 Jumping out of bed, John's clothes were nowhere to be found.
3 She planned how she should address the directors' meeting lying in the bath.
4 I was interested by the way the film showed some very interesting views of New Zealand.
5 Born in 1976, his childhood was spent in London.
6 I am assured that the film is based on the honest truth.
7 The first night of this play was a very unique experience.
8 The Irish Free State had held out the olive branch but nothing concrete had come of it.

5 Experiment by trying to write one of the ideas below. Compare your experiments with those of other students in the class.

- a video review that uses humour to make a serious point
- a book review which opens with a provocative question
- a review of the work of a film actor which is based on an unusual comparison
- a review of a light-hearted children's story which treats it as deeply serious literature
- a review of a song which relates it to some personal experience of your own

Positive and negative words

Some words have strong positive associations in English whereas others have negative associations. Thus, if someone says that a comedy at the theatre was *hilarious* you can be sure that they enjoyed it; if, however, their comment is that it was *ridiculous*, it is clear that they found it merely silly.

6 ↗◦ Below are a number of adjectives which might appear in reviews. Decide if they are positive or negative.

absurd   brilliant   captivating   disgraceful   dynamic
engrossing   exhilarating   fascinating   first-rate   grotesque
impressive   inspiring   invaluable   irritating   ludicrous
self-conscious   self-indulgent   shameful   stimulating
tasteful   tedious

7 ↗◦ Work with a partner and decide what the speaker is probably talking about in the following statements. Also decide whether the speaker is expressing an opinion that is basically positive or negative.

Example: 1 a book, positive

1 I was so engrossed that I literally couldn't put it down.
2 Jack interprets the lyrics in an unusual but rather captivating way.
3 Most of the shooting was done on location and they certainly used some impressive sites.
4 Although the decor is tasteful, the choice is restricted and the service slow and rather unsmiling.
5 It is a sensitive and inspiring approach to a difficult subject and is certainly worth waiting up for.
6 For a still-life it is remarkably dynamic.
7 Although I find his work rather self-indulgent, I am still intrigued by his use of alliteration, rhythm and rhyme.
8 The costumes and props are amateurish and at times rather absurd but the lines, on the whole, are well-delivered.

8 Work with a partner and choose five or six of the words from activity 6 that were new to you and that you would like to learn. Note something that you both feel could be appropriately described by that adjective, e.g. *first-rate – X's performance on TV last night.*

Giving opinions

There are many different ways of presenting your opinion in a piece of written work. You can use, for instance:

- *I* + verb, e.g. *I think, I consider, I believe … .*
- an adjective or adverb + adjective combination, e.g. *The film is (highly) amusing, wildly inaccurate.*
- a phrase, e.g. *in my opinion, to my mind, from my brother's point of view …*
- an adverb which indicates opinion, e.g. *undoubtedly, surprisingly, confusingly*
- a statement beginning *it is …* following by an adjective and, frequently, a clause with *should*, e.g. *It is disgraceful that such a film should be made.*
- an adverb + past participle combination, e.g. *The film is well produced, badly acted, appallingly directed.*

9 🔑 **Complete these sentences with one word only.**

1 Such roles, ... my mind, are likely to occur once in a lifetime.
2 .... my opinion, the play deserved its rave reviews.
3 I can't agree .... people who have admired his previous work.
4 As far as my mother was ...., the play was utterly ridiculous.
5 .... I see it, there are two main types of popular films.
6 From the point of .... of the audience, the performance is far too long.
7 It is my .... that James Wolf will turn out to be one of the great actors of the future.
8 Generally ...., the play was well acted.

10 🔑 **Match the adverb on the left with the adjective or participle on the right with which it has the strongest collocation.**

Example: *1 profoundly moving*

1	profoundly	improved
2	excruciatingly	developed
3	deeply	formed
4	eagerly	moving
5	admirably	deserved
6	considerably	dressed
7	impeccably	disappointing
8	richly	awaited
9	perfectly	exciting
10	highly	boring
11	wildly	honest

11 As a class, choose one or more examples of each of the things in the list. Try to select examples which are familiar to as many students as possible. Write the names of the selected songs, films, TV programmes etc. on the board.

- a song that is currently popular
- a film which is on in your town at the moment
- a TV programme which has recently been shown
- a book which you have read in English
- an old film
- a recent sporting event
- a popular singer or group
- a book which you use to help you learn English

Write sentences expressing your opinion about as many of the things or people listed on the board as possible. Try to use different ways of giving your opinion.

Take each of the things or people listed on the board in turns and compare the opinion sentences written by different students in the class. How much do you all agree with each other's opinions?

Planning and writing

12 Plan a review of a film, TV programme, song or book which you have seen, heard or read recently. Aim to write a sentence or two indicating the content of the work under review and then to devote the rest of your review to giving your own personal opinion about the work. Write your review.

In groups read out your reviews in turn – replacing the name of the work being reviewed by, say, the word, *Cockadoodledoo*. Guess what the subject of each review was.

13 Choose one of the tasks from the beginning of the unit and plan your answer. Write the answer to the task you have chosen. Try to use the tips and techniques from this unit as you write your answer.

11

Brochures

The aim of this unit is to answer the following questions.
- What kind of brochure might CAE ask you to write?
- What are the characteristics of brochures and similar literature?
- What style is appropriate when writing a brochure?
- How can you make sure you correct your work efficiently?
- How can you effectively write promotional or publicity literature?
- How can you use idioms effectively?

Here are four CAE-type tasks requiring you to write brochures. Notice that a number of different words can be used to describe what is, basically, a brochure.

1 Your local area is keen to encourage foreign tourists. You have been asked to write a brochure to send to other countries in order to promote the area. You have been requested to pay particular attention to at least three of the following – landscape; local food and drink; leisure facilities; places of historical interest; transport. Write the brochure.

2 Your family is going abroad for a couple of months and you have contacted an agency which will help you to rent out your house or flat while you are away. The agency has asked you to write an information sheet about your home, describing what it is like, where it is situated, what its special positive features are and whom it would particularly suit. Write the information sheet.

3 You are interested in getting more English practice. With a group of friends, one or two of whom are native speakers of English, you have set up an English club in your town. You hold regular meetings – some fairly formal with visiting speakers, some more social – at which you speak English. You decide to try and attract more members by preparing a publicity leaflet about the club. The leaflet should provide all the necessary basic information about the club and how to join, it should point out the advantages of membership and it should describe some of the enjoyable activities which have already taken place. Write the leaflet.

4 You feel particularly strongly about an issue that is causing considerable discussion in your area. You decide to publicise your views by producing a pamphlet in which you lay out clearly what the issue is, why you feel as you do and why those with opposing views are, in your opinion, mistaken. Write the pamphlet.

The characteristics of brochures and similar literature

As the exam tasks on the previous page demonstrate, there are different kinds of brochures and they can even be called by different names. What they have in common is that they:
– are short.
– aim partly to inform people.
– aim also to attract customers or supporters.

1 ⊶ Read the four exam tasks carefully and answer the following questions about them.

a) What is the brochure referred to as in each case?
b) What information must each give?
c) What would each like to attract people to do?

2 ⊶ Look at the brochure on the opposite page and answer these questions.

1 What information is provided in the brochure?
2 What is it trying to attract people to do?
3 Which parts of the text are simply giving information?
4 How did the writer of this brochure try to interest readers? Think about general presentation and sentence structure, in particular.
5 Underline any words or expressions that are used with the aim more of attracting customers than simply informing.

What style is appropriate when writing a brochure?

One of the most striking things about the brochure on the opposite page – and about most effective brochures – is the visual presentation. Brochures often use photos, drawings, maps, tables, cartoons, text in different colours and so on in order to make their points in a more eye-catching way.

If you were designing a brochure in 'real life', it would be a good idea to use at least some of the visual techniques mentioned above. However, it is not easy to create these visual effects in the examination room.

MOMI — MUSEUM of the moving image

bfi on the South Bank

Lights... Cameras... Action... Come to the award-winning Museum of the Moving Image and discover the fascinating and magical world of film and television. Both a museum and an experience, MOMI is an exciting blend of entertainment and education with plenty of hands-on fun. Enjoy a magic lantern show, 'fly' over the Thames like Superman, be interviewed by Barry Norman or audition for a Hollywood screen test. Along the way you will meet MOMI's famous actor guides, including a 1930's Odeon usherette, Hollywood director and even a Russian guard – all on hand to encourage participation and provide more detailed information.

South Bank, Waterloo, SE1 8XT.
24hr recorded information Tel 071-401 2636.

OPENING TIMES
Open 7 days a week from 10.00am – 6.00pm.
Last admission 5.00pm.
Closed 24, 25 & 26 December.

ADMISSION PRICES

	Normal Admission Price	Special Offer Price	SAVE
Adult	£5.50	£4.00	£1.50
Child	£4.00	£3.00	£1.00
OAP	£4.00	£3.00	£1.00
Student	£4.70	£4.00	£0.70

NEAREST STATIONS
Waterloo, Waterloo East.
Waterloo, Embankment, Charing Cross.

Recommended visit time approximately 2 hours.

TOWER HILL PAGEANT

London's first dark ride museum

Step aboard a time-car at the award winning Tower Hill Pageant and relive 2000 years of London's history. See, hear and smell the past as you travel through 27 lifelike scenes. Meet the Romans, Saxons and Vikings, smell the horrible plague and escape the terrors of the blitz. New in 1994 is a scene depicting the recent Docklands development.

Complementing the dark-ride is the walk-through Waterfront Finds Museum, with over 1000 exciting discoveries. Displays include a replica Roman ship, medieval jewellery and even a bubonic plague skeleton. The Tower Hill Pageant is one of London's most fascinating attractions, located just a raven's glide from the Tower of London.

Tower Hill, EC3N 4EE. Tel 071-709 0081.

OPENING TIMES
Open 7 days a week.
1 April to 31 October 9.30am – 5.30pm.
1 November to 31 March 9.30am – 4.30pm.
Closed 25 December.

ADMISSION PRICES

	Normal Admission Price	Special Offer Price	SAVE
Adult	£5.45	£3.50	£1.95
Child (4–15)	£3.45	£2.00	£1.45
OAP	£3.45	£2.00	£1.45
Student	£3.45	£2.00	£1.45

NEAREST STATIONS
Fenchurch Street, London Bridge.
Tower Hill

Recommended visit time approximately 1 hour.

---

sci√m — SCIENCE MUSEUM LONDON

Spaceships, aeroplanes, computers, and even an Egyptian mummy are among the many thousands of objects in the Science Museum's world famous collections. An exciting combination of actual equipment, instruments and machinery along with sets, drama characters and a range of special events tell the story of science, technology and medicine. Popular galleries include the Exploration of Space, Land Transport and Flight, which houses

many of the aircraft that made aviation history. Over 600 working exhibits encourage the visitor to experience science and technology "hands-on." In the interactive gallery Launch Pad, you can build a bridge, be a human battery, operate a model grain pit and lots more. Flight Lab offers exhibits that encourage you to test the principles of flight.

Exhibition Road SW7 2DD Tel: 071-938 8008/8080.

OPENING TIMES
Open Monday to Saturday from 10.00am – 6.00pm.
Sunday 11.00am – 6.00pm.
Closed 24, 25 & 26 December.

ADMISSION PRICES

	Normal Admission Price	Special Offer Price	SAVE
Adult	£4.50	£3.00	£1.50
Child	£2.40	£1.65	£0.75

NEAREST STATION
South Kensington.

Recommended visit time approximately 2 – 2½ hours.

3 🔑 **Work with a partner and decide whether the statements below are true or false.**

1 Turning the page round so that it is longer than it is high and then folding it into three and writing in three columns (like the brochure on the previous page and many other brochures). In this way you help yourself to get into the spirit of writing a brochure and so get into an appropriate style more easily.

2 By using the page in the way described above, it is easier to end up writing far fewer than 250 words without realising it.

3 If you are going to add drawings to your brochure in the exam, you must be able to draw good ones.

4 Drawing quick pictures and / or maps to illustrate your brochure will make it look more realistic and so will impress the examiner.

5 You would lose marks by simply writing the text of the brochure without paying any attention to the specific visual presentation which is characteristic of a brochure.

6 Using different coloured pens may make your work look more like a brochure but it is basically a waste of valuable time in the exam.

7 If you are asked to provide basic factual information about, for instance, opening times or how to get somewhere, it is essential that this information should be as complete and as accurate as possible.

4 🔑 **On the opposite page there are some more extracts from brochures. Which of the following techniques have been used to make what the writers are trying to sell sound attractive?**

catchy slogans   promises of a bargain   pictures in words
addressing the reader personally   examples of personal experiences
imperatives   exaggeration   plenty of adjectives   questions

5 **Work with a partner and discuss how the techniques in activity 4 could be used when writing answers to the four tasks at the beginning of the unit.**

6 🔑 **Underline any words and expressions in the extracts opposite which you think are used specifically to help attract customers.**

Write sentences of your own, which could be used in an answer to one of the tasks at the beginning of the unit. Try to use the words and expressions you have underlined.

1

A Giant Leap for Mackind!

Don't miss this year's **Mac Exhibition** at Olympia from Oct 11–15.

2

Travelling to London by rail couldn't be simpler. With regular services to two main stations, you'll be delivered to the heart of the capital. And when you buy a One Day Travelcard, you'll be able to visit any of the attractions featured in this brochure without having to buy extra tickets.

3

*Whether you are planning a shopping trip, visiting friends or relatives, going on holiday or simply off to see the sights, **Apex** is the ticket for you. You will need to book at least 7 days in advance, although the further ahead you book (up to 8 weeks) the better because these value for money tickets are very popular.*

4

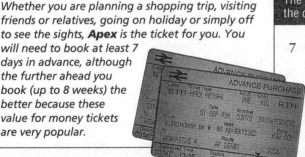

Have you ever wanted to get away from it all without having to spend hours travelling out of London?

5

Join Robin Hood in the world's greatest medieval adventure at **The Tales of Robin Hood.** Discover how the legend has grown over 700 years and search for the real Robin Hood by riding through the magical greenwood. Escape the Sheriff's deadly arrows and discover the sights and sounds of medieval England. The fascinating exhibition contains clues from the country's leading experts to help you explore the life of Robin Hood.

6

Where can you visit with a Rail Rover?

The following pages will tell you more about the different types of **Rail Rover** ticket...

7

Jane Simmons says: 'It's time we had a change of local government. Life has got much worse since these people have been in power. They should be spending money on schools and on local transport rather than on building new car parks and sports halls. I'll certainly be voting for the Workers' Party next time.'

8

With over 900 years of maritime and trading history, King's Lynn retains an ancient and unruffled charm. Wealth generated as long ago as the 12th century has left a fascinating legacy of beautiful and historic buildings. Carved wooden doorways facing cobbled streets, elegant courtyards and secret alleys remain unchanged for hundreds of years.

Using idioms

EXAM TIP

It is very easy to use idioms too frequently in a foreign language. It is better to avoid them totally, particularly in an exam, if you are not absolutely sure of what they are and how they are used. Idioms are fixed expressions and if just one word is wrong, then the sentence will sound peculiar and will not convey the meaning you wanted it to. If you use it in the wrong context, then your English will not sound natural.

7 🔊 Work with a partner and discuss these questions.

1 When do you think idioms are most used – in speech or in writing?
2 Look at the titles of the units in this book. In which of these text types, do you think native speakers might be most likely to use idioms?
3 Can you think of any other types of writing where idioms are commonly found?

8 🔊 Here are some quite common idioms. But which word do you need to complete them? Choose A, B, C or D.

1 You could dash off to London *at the drop of a* ....
A hat   B shoe   C pin   D coin

2 But if you are not already convinced, we have one more .... *up our sleeve.*
A arm   B hand   C card   D gun

3 Our products *knock* .... *off* anything you can buy in other shops.
A stripes   B spots   C lines   D dots

4 You won't need *to burn the midnight* .... if you purchase our miracle new study system.
A candle   B fire   C lamp   D oil

5 The Chamber of Horrors at Madame Tussaud's is guaranteed *to make your* .... *creep.*
A flesh   B feet   C skin   D body

6 The children will be *as good as* .... if you take them to the zoo.
A mice   B brass   C gold   D grass

7 Discover the .... *and byways* of England.
A lanes   B roads   C highways   D motorways

8 The hotel is just *a* .... *throw* from the beach.
A plate's   B ball's   C rock's   D stone's

9 ☞ Here are some sentences where the idiom has not been used accurately and needs correction. Make the corrections.

1 The hotel is attractively situated *off the beaten path*.
2 No words can *be justice to* the beauty of the surroundings.
3 The beauties we have described are just *the top of the iceberg*.
4 This brochure can only *rub the surface* of the wonders to be found in the museums of Paris.
5 Only *once in the blue moon* does one find such a heavenly spot.
6 We have a representative in every hotel ready to *jump attendance* on you, should you require it.
7 By taking one of our two-centre holidays you can, as it were, *kill two birds with one bullet*.
8 You can go to a tropical island *on the spur of the second*!
9 We guarantee that the holiday will *live on to your expectations*.
10 I don't think we're *letting the cat out of a bag* by telling you that the hotel has the best private beach on the island.
11 Our staff will *take out all the stops* to make your trip a success.
12 Our company never *lets the grass grow under our sandals*.

Correcting errors

10 ☞ There are twenty errors in this student's rather poor attempt at writing a leaflet. Underline all the mistakes that you find. Use the correction code on page 14 to indicate what kind of mistake has been made. Then correct the mistakes.

I am writting this leaflet because I want that everyone know what a wonderful town I live in. Not many people lives here and so it is a quite and peaceful place. Many visitors come here for relax and recover after an illness.

Many famous people visited this town. For example, Julia Roberts, David Copperfield and Elizabeth Taylor have all come here last year. They were feeling badly when they arrived but they soon stopped to feel ill here.

The town is surrounded with high mountains and you can breath a wonderful fresh air. If you feel fit, you can rent a bycicle and go for a ride into the mountains. If you will come in winter, you will be able to skiing.

Some people may wonder what is there to do in the evenings in a such small town. But there are several fine restaurants and clubs and the night-life is really unexpected good.

We are looking forward to see you when you will come to visit us.

STUDY TIP

You will get a much better mark in the exam and you will write better English in 'real life' too if you get into the habit of correcting your work. It is easier to make neat corrections if you allow plenty of space between the lines. In the exam it is a good idea to write on alternate lines so that you can correct your work without making it messy or difficult for the examiner to read.

11 Look back over some recent writing you have done and which your teacher has corrected. What kind of mistakes do you tend to make?

STUDY TIP

If you do seem to make mistakes in one particular area, then decide how you are going to help yourself improve. You could, for example, read your notes on the topic, read through the sections about it in a grammar book, do some practice exercises, work together with a classmate who has the same problem or ask your teacher for some other suggestions appropriate for your particular situation.

Planning and writing

12 Choose one of the tasks from the beginning of the unit and plan your answer. Write the answer to the task you have chosen. Try to use the tips and techniques from this unit as you write your answer.

12

Competition entries

The aim of this unit is to answer the following questions.

– What kind of competition entry might CAE ask you to write?

– What are the characteristics of competition entries and why does the exam ask you to write them?

– What are the main points dealt with in this book?

– How can you demonstrate that you have a range of English at your command?

– How can you use words in an accurate and appropriate way?

– How can you do your best on the day of the exam?

Competition entries are often used in CAE tasks. They are not really a distinct task type, of course, in the way that, say, a report or a note is. They usually, in fact, involve writing one of the other text types that we have practised in this book – an article, for example, or a review.

The four tasks below give you some idea of the kind of competition entry that you might be asked to write in CAE Paper 2.

1 You see this announcement of a competition in a young people's magazine.

Would you like to be a journalist for a day?

● *Where would you like to go?*
● *What would you like to report on?*
● *Who would you interview and what would you ask?*
● *What would make your report really special?*

We shall give free press passes to a selection of sporting, musical and other events to the person who writes the best answer to these questions.

Write an entry for the competition.

2 You see this announcement in an international student magazine.

SHORT STORY COMPETITION

We are looking for new talented short story writers whose work we shall include in an anthology of international student writing. Write us a short story which in some way relates to the particular experience of being a school, college or university student in the modern international world. Stories should be about 250 words in length.

You decide to enter the competition. Write a short story.

3 You see the following advertisement in a newspaper.

Would you like some money for a worthy cause? Perhaps something to help medical research? Or children? Or homeless people?

$750,000 to be given to a charity of your choice.

All you have to do is write to us to explain which charity you would choose and why. You should also describe how the money might be spent if it were given to the charity in question.

Send your entries to ...

Write your entry for the competition.

4 You see this notice in your workplace magazine.

- **What makes a good or a bad boss?**
- **What have you learnt about being a boss from your experience in this or any other company?**
- **What advice would you give to would-be bosses?**
- **What kind of boss do you think that you would make and why?**

We don't promise to promote you but we will send the person who submits the best set of answers to all of these questions on a management training course at an appropriate level. A selection of the best answers will also be published.

Write your entry for this competition.

Why does **CAE** often ask you to write competition entries?

The exam often asks you to write a competition entry because this gives you an authentic reason for writing as well as you can. The only thing that is special about writing a competition entry in real life is that you are showing off with your writing in a way that you do not bother to do when you are writing an informal letter or a note, for example. In an exam, of course, you need to make a good impression with any kind of writing you do, even if it is 'only' a note or a letter to a close friend.

As already mentioned a competition entry is not a distinct text type in itself. It can involve writing a text of a number of different types.

1 ⚬ Look at the four tasks at the beginning of this unit. Which of the text types practised in the different units of this book are you really being asked to write? In other words, which units, apart from this one, would help you in answering each of these tasks?

Revision exercises

It is necessary – if you are aiming to win the prize in the competition – to make good use of all the skills which you have worked on in this book. So in this section of the unit, you will practise a number of the points we have discussed – identifying the key aspects of the task, the value of planning your answers and the importance of both first and final impressions.

2 ⚬ Work with a partner and complete the table for the four tasks at the beginning of the unit.

Task	Who are you writing for?	What are you expected to cover?
1		
2		
3		
4		

3 Imagine that the four tasks at the beginning of the unit make up the section of the paper you are sitting. (This, of course, would never actually happen, as CAE does not have more than one competition entry on any one paper.) Work with a partner and discuss which task would be best for each of you. Why? Would any of the tasks be very difficult for you to answer? Why?

4 Work with a partner and discuss how you would plan answers to two of the four tasks at the beginning of the unit. Write paragraph headings – four or five – for each of the tasks. Then compare your plans with those of other pairs of students.

5 **Continue the sentences below in any logical way.**

1 I would take a tape recorder to the interview in case ....
2 As long as .... I think I'd make a good boss.
3 No sooner .... arrived at the college ....
4 I would make an excellent boss although ....
5 My first boss was very difficult to work for whereas ....
6 My current boss works as if ....
7 My current boss works like ....
8 I would donate the money to research into cancer despite the fact that ....
9 A good boss means that employees enjoy their work more. Moreover, ...
10 I would give my money to medical research. Eventually ....
11 I should very much like to interview Arnold Schwarzenegger. However, ...
12 I think the money should go towards research into heart disease. Alternatively, ...
13 Jack is good at dealing with people but not very efficient with his correspondence. Milly, conversely, ...
14 She was very successful as deputy manager. As a result, ...

6 Work with a partner and write a good opening sentence and a bad opening sentence for one of the tasks at the beginning of the unit. Be prepared to explain why the sentences are either good or bad, in your opinion.

Read your two opening sentences to the class without telling them which is the 'bad' and which is the 'good' one. Do they make the right choice? And do they have the same reasons for their choice as you do?

7 🖝 Work with a partner and think of ten words or phrases which can come in useful when writing an ending to a piece of work. Think about different text types – articles, reports, letters, reviews, narrative etc. Then compare your ideas with those of other students.

Demonstrating a range of English

EXAM TIP

When you write a competition entry, you particularly want to create a good impression. In an exam you also want to make a good impression whatever you are writing. You can set about doing this by using varied vocabulary and a range of sentence structures. Be careful, however, not to take risks in the exam. It is safer to write what you know is correct.

8 🖝 Work with a partner and discuss each of the six texts below. Although they are grammatically correct , they are not stylistically very special and do not demonstrate the 'range' which the CAE examiner is looking for. What is the problem with each of them? How can they be improved so that they would get a better mark for range?

1

I woke up early. I couldn't go back to sleep. I got dressed. I went for a walk. There was no-one else about.

2

If I won the competition, I would buy a new car. If there were any money left over, I would spend it on travel. I would enjoy travelling more if I went with someone else. So if there wasn't too much money left over, I would spend it on a holiday for two somewhere nearby rather than go somewhere more exotic on my own.

3

I made a lot of mistakes when I first started learning English. I made mistakes with the grammar, of course, and I made lots of mistakes with spellings. But I made most mistakes of all with pronunciation.

4

The room was very crowded with lots of different pieces of furniture in it.

5

Edinburgh is a very nice place to visit. It's a beautiful city with lots of good places to see and there are good things to do in the evening too.

6

There was a lot to see from the windows as the train travelled through the country.

Using words accurately and appropriately

Always take care with your choice of words. Even native speakers can get tied up in their use of English!

9 🖛0 **Work with a partner and discuss what problems have arisen because of careless use of language. Then rewrite the sentences so that it is absolutely clear what is meant.**

1 (From *Camera Weekly*) p. 74 Diary: Where to shoot kids singing carols in a courtyard and the best guide to photogenic country walks.

2 In another answer in Parliament, it was disclosed that 12,500 male prisoners are having to share a cell.

3 Mr Ronald Brown (Edinburgh, Labour) said the Government had been complacent too long. Floating voters would expect coastal waters to at least meet the standard of the average European country.

4 Police seized 1,500 rare birds' eggs from a house in Mosborough, Sheffield. A man has been questioned about a suspected poaching operation.

5 Lloyd – a senior executive with Carlton Greeting Cards – was posted to England.

6 Three boys escaped when a wall collapsed at the Zoological Gardens, Regent's Park.

7 Following the ceremony, a small reception was staged round a fire on the beach during which the guests toasted the happy couple.

8 Both experienced and novice bell-ringers interested in joining the group are invited to the church on Monday September 22nd at 8 p.m. when experienced bell-ringer, Ian Harris, will get the group off the ground.

On the day of the exam

10 Work in groups of three or four students. What tips would you give to a CAE candidate who asks you *How can I make sure of getting the best possible marks on the day of the exam?* Make notes of all the tips which your group comes up with.

Compare your tips with those of other groups. Did they think of things which you forgot or vice versa? Do any of their tips conflict with yours? If so, which tips do you think are better?

Look at the advice given on the next page. Did you think of everything on this page? Did you come up with anything more that could be added to these tips?

Planning and writing

To pass the CAE Writing Paper, you need, of course, to demonstrate that you are able to write correct English at a suitably advanced level.

11 Write an answer to one of the tasks from the beginning of the unit. You will probably want to use one of the plans you prepared for this task in activity 4 – unless you have had some new ideas since then. Make sure you organise your writing logically and that you begin and end your work in an effective way.

When you have finished writing, look at your work with a critical eye. Check particularly carefully for:

– agreement of subject and verb.
– verb tenses.
– prepositions.
– word order.
– spelling.
– any errors that you know you are personally prone to make.

Correct any mistakes that you find. Then exchange work with a partner and read one another's work critically. Discuss any errors that you think you find in each other's writing and correct your work if you feel that your partner is right in his or her criticism.

Ask your teacher to correct your work. Pay particular attention to any mistakes which the teacher finds but which both you and your partner overlooked.

On the day of the exam – remember these tips

A Planning your answers

Read the tasks you have chosen very carefully. Pay attention to what the task tells you about:

- **who** you are writing to – this will help you to choose an appropriate style.
- **why** you are writing – this will help you to decide what to write.
- **what kind of text** you are writing – this will help you to choose an appropriate format and layout.
- **all the requirements** of the task (usually two or three things) – this will help you to plan your answer.

Allow plenty of time for planning your answers – to make sure that you cover all the points asked for in the question in a logical, well-ordered way.

B Timing

Time your answers well. You may decide to devote a little more time to Section A but make sure you leave at least 50 minutes for planning, writing and checking your Section B answer.

C Section B choice

Choose the Section B task which you feel you can do best. Remember that you must have the range of vocabulary needed to write a good answer. You also need to be able to answer all the different parts of the task.

The task you can do best may not be the most interesting question.

D The wording of the question

In Section A, don't just copy large chunks of the question as it is easy to do this in an inappropriate way. Try to use your own words when this is possible – this will get you better marks.

If you do need to use words that are in the question – and you certainly will sometimes – make sure you don't make spelling mistakes with words that are printed on the paper. This creates a very bad impression.

E Presentation and layout

Plan the layout of your answer before you start writing.

Don't waste time rewriting your answers.

Make it clear where one paragraph ends and the next begins – either indent or leave an extra line between paragraphs.

Make your handwriting as clear as possible – don't use a very light pen and remember that very small or careless handwriting can be difficult for examiners to read.

F Correcting your work

Allow plenty of time for checking your work and, if necessary, correcting it.

Write on alternate lines of the paper – this makes it easier to make corrections.

Make corrections neatly – score out once or use correcting fluid carefully.

G Remember

Examiners will be thinking about six different aspects of your work and asking themselves the following questions.

Accuracy:	How accurate is your writing?
Content:	Have you answered all the parts of the question?
Organisation:	Is your work well ordered, in clear linked paragraphs?
Range:	Have you used a range of vocabulary and sentence structure?
Register:	Have you written in an appropriately formal or informal style?
Target reader:	Would your writing have the desired effect on the reader?

H Remember

This book has given you a lot of guidance about how to write well in English. In the few days before the exam, look through the work you have done in this book so that it is fresh in your mind on the day of the examination.

Good Luck!

Answer key

Unit 1   Foundation unit

1 1 Two hours.
   2 Two.
   3 250 words for each of the two questions, i.e. 500 words in all.
   4 All candidates must answer the first question (Section A) but can then choose one of four in Section B.
   5 No, all questions carry the same potential marks.

3

Task	Kind of writing	Purpose of writing	Intended readership
Section A, task i	article	to report on opinion survey results, to inform readers	members of local English club
Section A, task ii	note	to invite members to meeting, to encourage them to bring ideas	members of local English club
Section B, task 1	review	to share opinions and critically assess a book or film	editors selecting new reviewers; also, indirectly, magazine readers
Section B, task 2	brochure, i.e. leaflet	to publicise company	young people in other countries
Section B, task 3	informal letter	to inform	Australian penfriend
Section B, task 4	report	to complain, to make suggestions	management of sports centre

4 – *Relevance* means points that are appropriate for an answer to the particular question asked.
   – *Layout* refers to the way the answer is positioned on the page.
   – *Cohesive devices* are words and expressions used by a writer to show the connections between sentences and paragraphs. Examples include *however*, *on the other hand*, *this explains why*.
   – *Register* here means a style of English that is appropriate for the particular social circumstances, e.g. formal or informal.
   – The *target reader* is the person or people who the question presents as the future reader(s) of the piece of writing. In task 1 on page 8, for example, the editors or readers of the magazine (rather than the examiners) are the target readers.
   – *Non-impeding errors* are mistakes which don't result in the reader being unsure what the writer means. Spelling *bicycle* as *bycicle* would not cause anyone any confusion whereas using

as soon as when you mean *as long as* would create difficulties in understanding for the reader.

– *Omissions* are things which are not done. Here it refers particularly to parts of the question which are ignored in the answer.

5 1 2 marks.
   2 No mark.
   3 No, your work does not have to be grammatically perfect to get 5 marks.
   4 The language is natural and shows a good range.
   5 Yes, a piece of writing has to be clearly organised to get 3 marks.
   6 'Conventions' refer to the things that are standard about the format of a formal letter, e.g. writer's address in top right hand corner, opening *Dear Sir* and closing *Yours faithfully*, or opening *Dear Mrs Brown* and closing *Yours sincerely*. See Unit 3 for more details about letter-writing conventions.

6 a) 4   b) 1   c) 5   d) 3   e) 6
   f) 2

7 Student A's work got 5 marks. Student B's work got 3 marks. Student A does exactly what the question asks, uses English accurately with a good range of expressions and structures. Student B does exactly what the question asks but makes quite a lot of mistakes even though they do not stop the reader from understanding what is meant, e.g. *writting, One of this, I'm looking forward to hear.*

8 I <u>have been able to</u> swim ever since I <u>was</u> a small child and <u>people say</u> I am a very good swimmer. Most of all I enjoy <u>swimming in</u> the sea. Most weekends <u>I go</u> to the beach which is about 30 kilometres <u>away</u> from my home. One day when I arrived <u>at</u> this beach it was so <u>crowded</u> that I decided to walk further along the beach than <u>usual</u>. Soon I came to a <u>delightful</u> little cove that was <u>surprisingly</u> deserted. I saw a sign <u>which / that</u> said 'For naturists only' and I thought that meant the beach was <u>only for</u> nature-lovers.

Unit 2   Writing based on a reading task

1

Task	Kind of writing	Purpose of writing	Intended readership
Unit 2, task 1	letter	to complain about inaccurate article, to correct errors	editor, readers of newspaper
Unit 2, task 2 i	report	to explain why one candidate was selected and others were not	club committee members
Unit 2, task 2 ii	letter	to announce committee's decision	unsuccessful applicant for sponsorship

2 The points listed below are relevant. The others are not obviously relevant.

Unit 1, Section A, task ii
   – details regarding time and place of the meeting
   – the fact that there will be tea and biscuits
   – statement of aims of meeting
   – reminder to bring ideas about new members' campaign to meeting

Unit 2, task 1
   – correction of all the mistakes in the article
   – request for a printed apology and correction of the mistakes
   – statement of your nationality and fact that you took part on course
   – an outline of how one student broke his / her leg
   – a hope that the summer school will continue in future years

Unit 2, task 2 i
- name of person you chose
- reasons favouring your choice
- weaknesses of three candidates not chosen
- strengths of three candidates not chosen

Unit 2, task 2 ii
- statement of who got the sponsorship
- expression of regret that sponsorship could not be offered to this candidate
- encouragement for applicant to try other sources for sponsorship

3 Here are some possible reasons for rejecting these points.

Unit 1, Section A, task ii
- summary of article – already known to readers
- reminder to bring proposals for next year's programme to be discussed at meeting – in article already

Unit 2, task 1
- an accusation that the editor was lying – too rude
- description of what Canchester is like as a town for foreign visitors – too general, would distract from main point of letter
- an attack on modern journalism – too rude

Unit 2, task 2 i
- statement that you could not make a choice and pass decision back to committee – not doing what you are asked to do
- decision to split sponsorship money between all four candidates short-listed – not appropriate as solution to problem
- greetings to fellow committee members – not appropriate for a report

Unit 2, task 2 ii
- statement of problem regarding candidate's dress, e.g. dirty fingernails at interview – too specific, could be offensive
- full explanation as to why successful candidate was chosen – too specific

4 Unit 1, Section A, task i – 2, 4
Unit 1, Section A, task ii – 4, 5
Unit 2, task 1 – 1, 3, 4, 5, 6
Unit 2, task 2 i – 2, 3, 4
Unit 2, task 2 ii – 4, 6

5 1 It is probably a good idea to allow more time for Section A as there is so much more to read in Section A and it is important to think particularly carefully about the content of your answer in the light of the reading input. Discuss it further with your teacher if you are unsure about how suitable it is for you personally.
2 Do not simply skim the task. You must read the task fully or you may miss out important aspects of your answer.
3 Underlining or highlighting is probably a good idea to help you focus on what is really important in the question.
4 It is only a good idea to copy phrases directly from the input if you can do so in a relevant and totally grammatical way – it is easy to give the examiners the impression that you are only copying bits from the reading input because you are not quite sure what it means. Of course, there are sure to be details that you do have to copy but it is generally better to use your own words wherever possible.
5 The order in which you do the sections is purely a matter of personal preference.
6 It is a good idea to check spellings. It infuriates examiners to see words which are written correctly on the exam paper misspelt in candidates' work.

6 Some possible answers are suggested below.

2 It is not true to say that arts events were <u>infrequent</u>.
3 It is unfair to suggest that <u>not many of the students were really interested in attending lessons</u>.
4 Some students <u>went so far as to request additional language lessons one evening a week</u>.
5 <u>Our town has benefited enormously from the dedicated work which TR has carried out with elderly people over the last forty years</u>.
6 SM is <u>a respected and successful academic</u>.
7 DO's <u>wife is currently a housewife taking care of their three-year-old daughter</u>.
8 AS <u>was unassuming in manner but clearly has considerable intellectual ability</u>.

8 Some possible answers are suggested below.

Function	Writing to a close friend	Writing to a stranger
Thanking for present	Thanks for the great book – love the cartoons.	Thank you for the most enjoyable and amusing book you sent me.
Requesting a favour	Could you possibly do me a favour? We're doing a school project and I'd be really grateful for some help with it.	I was wondering if there might be any chance of your giving me some assistance with a project I am currently working on?
Making a suggestion	How about meeting at the theatre next Saturday?	Would it be convenient for you if we were to meet at the theatre next Saturday?
Apologising	I'm terribly sorry I forgot to post you the report.	I must apologise for omitting to post you the report. It was inexcusable of me.
Complaining	I wish your boys would stop playing their stereo so loud in the evenings. It really gets on my nerves.	I would be very grateful if you could ensure that your sons turn their music down after 11 p.m.
Initial salutation	How's life? All's well, I hope.	I hope that you and your family are keeping well.
Drawing letter to a close	Better go now or I'll miss the post. Longing to see you soon. Love,	I look forward to your reply. With very best wishes, Yours sincerely,

9 None of the quoted sentences is polite or tactful enough.

1 As it is club members who will be reading the article they are likely to be rather offended by the tone of this sentence and so will be even less prepared to help out.

2 This sentence may be intended to be amusing but it is more likely to cause offence.

3 This sentence is too colloquial for such a task and sounds rude.

4 This sentence is too extreme. It is very unlikely to be appropriate to threaten solicitors in a CAE writing task – although candidates regularly do so.

5 It is usually better to <u>imply</u> that someone is lying rather than to say so directly.

6 This report is read by the committee members who decided on the short-list and they will consider that their judgement is being criticised by a comment like this. This sort of comment is, therefore, likely to irritate them.

7 TR would be understandably upset by a comment like this.

8 It may be true that SM was by far the best candidate but it could be upsetting to mention this to the unsuccessful candidates.

Unit 3   Letters

1 Most formal to least formal – 1, 3, 2, 4

3 A.

Formal. The underlined words and phrases as well as the full verb forms (rather than contractions) all serve to show that this is a formal letter.

<u>12 Loudon Road,</u>
<u>London</u>
<u>NW6 3AL</u>

Dear <u>Mr and Mrs</u> Winterspoon,

It is <u>with regret</u> that this has to be my first letter to you as our new neighbours.

Please <u>would you be so kind as to dissuade</u> your son from playing such loud music so late at night. My wife has <u>long</u> been <u>prone to suffer from</u>

insomnia and it is quite <u>intolerable</u> for her to have to <u>endure</u> such a cacophony until one o'clock every morning. If your son insists on playing records until so late, could he not at least <u>purchase</u> headphones so that others are not <u>inconvenienced</u>?

If your son <u>does not refrain</u> from such antisocial behaviour in the future, I shall <u>have no choice but to contact</u> the police.

<u>Yours sincerely,</u>
<u>David Fogey</u>

B

Informal. All the underlined words and phrases add an informal tone to the letter.

<u>Darling Jo,</u>
   <u>Hope</u> you had a <u>great</u> flight home and are missing me as much as I miss you. You will write soon and tell me all <u>you're getting up to, won't you?</u>
   <u>Things</u> have been <u>pretty grim</u> here since you left. <u>Just work</u> and more work. I suppose the neighbours are glad at least that I don't have music on every evening any more.
   <u>I'm moving ahead</u> with plans to come and see you one weekend next month. If I book now, I can get a cheap flight for the second <u>w/e</u> in the month. Would that be <u>OK</u> for you? I really <u>don't</u> want to wait any longer to see you again.
   <u>Drop me a line ASAP</u> and I'll <u>go ahead</u> and book a flight if you <u>just give me the word.</u>
<u>All my love,</u>
<u>Chris</u>

<u>XXXX</u>

4

Formal letters	Informal letters
– literary expressions	– phrasal verbs
– long sentences	– colloquial vocabulary
– full forms of verbs (*I would* etc.)	– the word *nice*
	– contractions (*I'd* etc.)
– carefully constructed sentences and paragraphs	– sentences that sound close to spoken English
– sentences that are clearly written rather than spoken English	– question tags
	– omission of subject of sentence

5 2 Informal. Formal – *I apologise for the delay in replying to your letter. This was due to pressure of work.*

3 Formal. Informal – *Do please write back to me soon. I'm longing to hear your news.*

4 Formal. Informal – *Please send me some info about villas I could rent on the Med.*

5 Informal. Formal – *How is the current situation? I hope that everything is satisfactory at present.*

6 Informal. Formal – *She maintains that he is a pleasant person but I cannot accept her point of view.*

7 Formal. Informal – *Ring me at the number I've given you.*

8 Informal. Formal – *I hope it will be convenient for you if we collect you at 6. That should allow us to arrive in time for some refreshments.*

6 Here are some ways of completing the sentences. There are other possibilities.

1 Thank you *for the lovely letter which I* received yesterday.

2 It was lovely *to see you again* last weekend.

3 I hope we *shall be able to get together* again soon.

4 I wish you *were* here with me.

5 I'm sorry I *haven't been in touch for such* a long time.

6 I must stop *now or I won't* catch the post.

7 Please *remember me to / give my regards to / give my best wishes to* your parents.

8 I'm looking forward *to hearing from you* soon.

7 1 response   2 apply   3 available
4 grateful   5 enclose   6 return
7 convenience   8 referees   9 reference
10 correction

8 Here is one possible way to answer this question.

Dear Mrs Jones,
   I hope you had a smooth and enjoyable flight home. We are missing you very much and look forward to hearing from you soon.
   Life has been quiet at home since you left and I am busy at work once more.
   I hope very much to be able to visit you soon. Would it be convenient if I were to come for the second weekend in June? Do please let me know if that does not suit you.
   If this would suit you, I'll book my flight, but

please do not hesitate to say if you have other arrangements for that weekend.

With all good wishes,
Christopher

9 1 talked into giving – *persuaded to give*
2 done up – *redecorated*
3 cut off – *isolated*; to be put up – *to be accommodated*
4 make up for – *compensate for*
5 were coming down with flu – *had caught flu (influenza)*; will have got over it – *will have recovered from it*
6 told me off – *reprimanded me*; setting up – *organising*; done in – *exhausted*
7 won't be put out – *won't be offended*; keep your talk down to – *limit your talk to*
8 brought out – *published*
9 look at – *consider*; picked up – *gained*

10 1 postponing – *putting off*; pondered – *thought over* or *thought through*
2 dissuade (your parents) from (wanting) – *talk (your parents) out of (wanting)*
3 raise – *bring up*
4 pretending – *making out*
5 persist with – *carry on / go on (studying or with your studies)*
6 Support – *Back up*; fulfil – *carry out*

11 Some possible plans are suggested below. There are, of course, many different possibilities.

1 – introduction – who you are, thanks for offer, accept offer
  – suggest programme
  – information about members
  – information about previous meetings
  – offer accommodation
  – conclusion – look forward to meeting etc.
2 – introduction – greetings etc.
  – sport at school
  – popular spectator sports
  – unusual traditional sports and games
  – recent changes
  – closing – best wishes etc.
3 – introduction – reference to offending article
  – information about why tourists can enjoy country
  – historical sights
  – more ideas for what is of interest to tourists – entertainments, sports facilities etc.
  – correction of errors in article
  – conclusion – request for letter to be printed to set the picture straight
4 – introduction – greetings etc.
  – benefits of travel
  – money – could earn some too
  – danger – reassure them etc.
  – closing – give own news in brief, best wishes etc.

Unit 4   Articles

Task	What is the aim of the article?	What do you know about the likely readers of the article?
2	to describe and make suggestions	people from a range of countries, interested in travel; possibly interested in choosing a honeymoon destination for themselves
3	to inform and give opinions	university students in another country, mainly young people; have some interest in international affairs
4	to amuse	people interested in your favourite hobby, with at least some background information about it; are enthusiastic about it.

2

> Similarity between writing an article and a letter: *style can be formal or informal*
>
> Contrasts between readers of letters and articles:
>
> Readers of letters:
> i) *are known to writer.*
>
> ii) *have a known amount of knowledge of subject of letter.*
> iii) *will read letter to end.*
>
> Readers of articles:
> *writer doesn't know exactly who they will be.*
> *have unknown degree of background information.*
> *won't necessarily read to end.*
>
> This means that an article should:
> i) *be written for a range of readers.*
> ii) *be interesting enough to catch and hold attention.*

5 Here are some of the techniques which the writer has used. You may well spot more.

- eye-catching title question in first paragraph
- addressing the reader directly
- painting pictures in words of the scene, e.g. sentence beginning *An island where casuarina pines …*
- some interesting facts about the island and the hotel
- attention to sounds as well as images in descriptions of island – contrast between sound of traffic and that of the birds that wake the visitor
- clear paragraphing
- use of interesting words rather than ordinary ones (*talcum powder sand* rather than, simply, *fine sand*, for instance)
- reference at the end back to something mentioned earlier on in article (Frederick Forsyth story)

6 1 G   2 D   3 C   4 H   5 B
   6 E   7 A   8 F

7 Here are some of the techniques used by the writers of the paragraphs. You may find other techniques which are also effective.

1 question; addressing the reader directly
2 direct statement of the situation; striking military metaphor in the use of the word *barrage*
3 statement of facts; surprising fact, perhaps, about the huge size of the Amazon Basin
4 setting of the scene; whetting of curiosity as rather strange details of the scene are mentioned (name of lounge, the mysterious

'small door', the 'nutrient cocktails' and their unusual names); use of quotation marks to show reader exactly what the expressions used in the bar are
5 exaggeration in first sentence; movement from the specific example to the general and then back to a specific example again
6 facts (surprising for a British reader, at least); questions including a puzzle question at the end
7 surprising facts; contrast with people's ignorance and the serious reality of the situation
8 direct personal situation; unusual facts of situation highlighted; ends on note referring to feeling rather than fact

8 1 b) is more emphatic. The unusual word order emphasises *spectacular*.
2 b) is more emphatic. The *did* (stressed when the sentence is spoken) emphasises *enjoyed*.
3 b) is more emphatic. The adverb *unexpectedly* adds emphasis to *successful*.
4 a) is more emphatic. The word order with inversion gives extra force to the sentence.
5 b) is more emphatic. It is what grammar books call a 'cleft sentence'. The introductory phrase is used to give extra emphasis to what comes later in the sentence.
6 a) is more emphatic. Using the modal *must* gives extra force to the sentence.

9 Some possible ways of rewriting the statements are suggested here. There are, of course, other correct answers.

1 – Luigi's must be the most exotic restaurant I have ever been to.

– The most exotic restaurant I have ever been to is Luigi's.

2 – I did enjoy the disco despite its deafening music.

 – I enjoyed the disco enormously despite the deafening noise.

3 – Never before have I seen such a spectacular sunset.

 – I have never before seen such a spectacularly dramatic sunset.

4 – The picturesque harbour is something that we shall always remember.

 – What we shall always remember is the picturesque harbour.

5 – We spent a truly memorable day climbing the highest mountain on the island.

 – It was the day when we climbed the highest mountain on the island that was the most memorable.

6 – James is undoubtedly one of the most intriguing people I have ever met.

 – James must be one of the most intriguing people I have ever met.

10 Some possible ways of completing the sentences are suggested below. There are, of course, many other correct answers.

1 Never have I been more afraid than *I was then, alone in the dark and lost.*

2 What I shall never forget is *the way he helped me when I needed him.*

3 The most exhilarating moment in my life was *standing on the top of the mountain above the clouds.*

4 I did enjoy *meeting your family last night.*

5 *St Petersburg* must be the most romantic place I have ever been to.

11 Here are some alternative words. There are many other possibilities.

1 exhilarating, romantic, relaxing, memorable, astonishing, remarkable

2 picturesque, spectacular, attractive, friendly, wonderful, heavenly

3 disastrous, catastrophic, unhappy, miserable, lonely, uncomfortable

4 kind, pleasant, good-natured, generous, warm, open-hearted

5 sunny, warm, mild, hot, perfect, delightful

6 unfriendly, rude, bad-tempered, disagreeable, incompetent, dishonest

12 Here are some possible plans.

2 Introductory paragraph – brief statement of where I live (own parents came here for honeymoon and decided to stay)
Paragraph 2 – what's romantic about it (historical association with poets etc, beautiful surrounding countryside etc.)
Paragraph 3 – places to go (historic areas, suggestions for country walks etc.)
Paragraph 4 – activities to enjoy (picnic on river, most romantic restaurants, open air dancing etc.)
Conclusion – make honeymoon as long as possible

3 Introductory paragraph – statement of where I'm from and the problem I want to discuss (unemployment)
Paragraph 2 – description of nature of problem and how it affects people's lives
Paragraph 3 – reasons for problem
Paragraph 4 – suggestions about how to minimise unemployment
Conclusion – why something must be done

4 Introductory paragraph – why I'd like to share this experience with readers
Paragraph 2 – background to experience, where I was, what I was doing etc.
Paragraph 3 – what exactly happened
Paragraph 4 – consequences
Conclusion – warning to others to avoid this situation

Below you have a suggestion as to how an article might be written in response to task 1.

Did you sometimes find it difficult to find things to do in your spare time last term? Were you often at a loose end wondering whether you were missing out on all the exciting events that must surely be going on somewhere or other?

You weren't alone. In fact, 93% of the students we interviewed said that they had been disappointed with the college's social programme. First year students, in particular, experienced difficulties meeting new people and spent more time than they would have liked alone in their rooms.

This term, however, things will be very different. An outstanding programme has been arranged by a new Social Events Committee. Their chairperson, Maria de

Souza, told me, 'We have some amazing things coming up. There'll be a film every Friday starting with the latest Schwarzenegger next week. Once a week on Wednesday there is going to be either a debate or a talk from an outside speaker. This Wednesday a world-famous mountaineer is coming to show us slides and tell us of his adventures.' Maria is also enthusiastic about some excursions which the college is organising on Sundays for students interested in exploring the countryside around the town. They will be for those who are up on time after the Saturday discos which are to take place in the college hall with disc jockeys from the local radio station.

Not only will these activities be enjoyable and interesting, they will also be a good way to meet your fellow-students. None will be beyond the pocket of the average hard-up student and, who knows, some of the debates and talks might even be of value to your studies.

So you won't need to spend your evenings alone in your room this term. Come along to these events and enjoy yourself. You'll certainly be seeing me there!

Unit 5   Narratives

2 Here are some possible elements for a good story.

- good characterisation
- a clear structure with a beginning, middle and end
- convincing dialogue
- an exciting incident
- original use of language
- an interesting idea
- humour
- suspense
- a surprise ending

3 The second version is more interesting as it creates a much more vivid picture of the incident – by setting the scene more precisely, by describing the characters' feelings, by building up the tension more.

4 **1** **Variety of tenses**
  a) Past simple.
  b) To set the background to a scene.

  c) To describe events that happened before the main events in the story.
  d) *Used to* or *would* can be used to describe past habits, for example.

2 **Direct speech**
  a) 'Our car's broken down. Could you possibly let us have a bucket of water for it?' and 'Don't touch my baby, don't touch my baby.'
  b) The men explained that their car had broken down and asked for a bucket of water for it. and She begged them not to touch her baby.
  c) It creates a much more vivid picture for the reader.

3 **Vivid verbs**
  a) shriek, dash, scream, emerge, snatch, grab

4 **Description of setting**
  a) The isolation of the house, the fact that there is no-one else nearby, the weather.
  b) It helps to create a more vivid picture for the reader and explains why the crime was possible; no-one was nearby to help, there was an easy escape route, the husband was not surprised that people asked for water for their car in such weather conditions.
  c) Probably not – too much detail can distract.

5 **Appeal to the five senses**
  a) Sight, hearing, taste, smell and touch.
  b) Sight (large garden bordering on park etc.), hearing (sounds of shrieks, slamming doors etc.) and touch (cold outside versus warmth inside etc.).
  c) There could have been references to, say, the smell and the taste of food and drink the characters had been enjoying.

6 **Reference to feelings**
  a) Six (not counting the police).
  b) We are not told anything about the feelings of the two burglars and we only know that the baby did not feel anything because he slept through the whole incident. We know that they were all warm and comfortable at the beginning of the story, that Anita and the narrator were terrified by the incident, that Ron was alarmed as the water was thrown over him and that they were all shocked by the incident.
  c) By their actions and reactions – Ron's shriek, for instance, the narrator's locking herself in the bathroom, Anita's screams,

their shivering at the end of the story. We are also told more directly about how they felt at the beginning and the end of the story.

d) There are many possible answers to this – perhaps we could have been told how they felt at losing certain objects which might have had a special sentimental value or whether they felt they immediately wanted to move to another house, for example.

e) Possible ways include: a direct statement of feelings; conveying feelings through quoting the characters' words; describing what people do can serve to convey feelings too (for example, if someone scratches their head, you know that they are puzzled); describing their appearance.

8 1 Not a good opening at all. It doesn't make it sound as if the writer is going to have an interesting story to tell.

2 Good – clearly lots of memorable things happened.

3 This is quite good. It makes it sound as if at least one day is worth reading about.

4 Excellent. An interesting opening which makes the reader want to know more.

5 It is unlikely that this sentence will turn out to be relevant. It certainly doesn't capture the reader's interest.

6 A basic factual opening. It sounds more appropriate for the beginning of a report than an article.

9 1 This sums up the story.

2 Surprise.

3 It relates back to opening sentence 2 in activity 8 with a reference to the flight at each end of the person's holiday.

4 This sums up the story.

5 Surprise.

6 It relates back to opening sentence 3 in activity 8, saying much the same thing in a different way.

10 Here are some more examples of alternatives to *say*.

'Please help me,' she begged.
'I'm cleverer than you,' he boasted.
'There's a fly in my soup,' she complained.
'I shall support James in the election,' he declared.
'You must do it this way,' she insisted.

'Your eyes are like stars,' he murmured.
'Bring me the papers this minute,' she ordered.
'I'll be home before midnight,' he promised.
'There's a mouse over there,' she shrieked.
'Don't be so ridiculous,' he snapped.
'P-p-p-lease h-h-help m-m-m-me,' she stammered.
'I'll stop your pocket money if you don't tidy your bedroom,' he threatened.
'You shouldn't go into the park after dark. It's dangerous,' she warned.
'Don't make a sound,' he whispered.

11 Some more examples of alternatives to *go* could be:

creep (crept, crept)	They crept into the house, trying hard not to wake their parents.
dash	He dashed to the station and just managed to jump on the train.
limp	Why are you limping? Did you fall when you were riding?
march	She marched into the office and demanded to see the manager.
plod	I plodded home laden with everything I'd bought for the party.
skip	The little girl skipped down the hill obviously without a care in the world.
stagger	The men had drunk so much wine that they could hardly stagger home.
stroll	On holiday we spent most of our evenings just strolling around the town looking in shop windows.

12 2 Tired cold people huddle in a corner to keep
warm.
3 Thunder rumbles in the distance.
4 Heavy traffic thunders past on a motorway.
(You can also say *Heavy traffic rumbles in
the distance.*)
5 Car tyres screech on wet roads.
6 A dissatisfied audience hisses at a poor
performance.
7 An old door creaks on its hinges.
8 Children giggle at a joke.
9 A nervous person trembles before speaking
in public.
10 A hungry person munches an apple.

Unit 6 Reports

1 A advertisement from a travel brochure – flowery
language, not objective in tone as a report
should be
B postcard or informal letter – informal
language, contractions, informal vocabulary,
informal sentence structure
C novel or short story – content is clearly fiction
D report – headings, formal factual style, factual
content

4 Report 1
1 Introduction – basic details of own
participation.
2 Travel arrangements
3 Study arrangements
4 Accommodation arrangements
5 Problems encountered
6 Conclusion – recommendations

Report 2
1 Introduction – the current situation in
Scotland
2 The main problem
3 Economic and social effects of unemployment
4 Causes of unemployment in Scotland today
5 Action currently being taken
6 Implications of Scottish unemployment for X
and Y Ltd

5 Here are possible plans. There are, of course,
other ways of approaching the tasks.

Report 3
Introduction – brief outline of proposed project
Fuller description of proposal
Reasons why it is a good idea

Improvements it would bring
Conclusion – request for official response

Report 4
Introduction – outline of self (age, nationality etc.
and languages known)
Description of how learnt (a) French and (b)
Russian
Strengths of methods used
Weaknesses of methods used
Future language learning plans

6 Title: Suitability of Camford as a Location for a
Language School
1 Introduction
2 Geographical factors
3 Facilities
4 Drawbacks
5 Conclusion

7 1 You usually indent the first line of the
paragraph, i.e. you begin your first sentence
about two centimetres in from the margin.
Some writers prefer to leave a line between
paragraphs, particularly in a report.
Whichever way you use, it is, however,
essential to make it absolutely clear where one
paragraph ends and the next begins.
2 Two to four. One-sentence paragraphs are
extremely rare, except perhaps in popular
journalism, and are usually considered bad
style. More than four, or perhaps five,
sentences in a paragraph would probably
make it too long.
3 Four to six.
4 The one that sums up the idea of the paragraph
– the rest of the paragraph usually explains or
illustrates the idea in that sentence.
5 It is frequently but certainly not always the
first sentence in the paragraph.

8 There is a line between paragraphs. There are
five paragraphs with two to four sentences in
them. The topic sentence is the first sentence in
each of the paragraphs in this report.

10 Secondly (to introduce the second point)
Moreover (to add another point)
nevertheless (to introduce a contrasting point)
First of all (to make a first point)
In addition (to add another point)
To conclude (to introduce a conclusion)
however (to introduce a proviso)

Notice that in the context of this report *however* and *nevertheless* could be interchanged.

11 1 nevertheless
2 furthermore, in addition
3 in conclusion, finally
4 finally, lastly, last but not least
5 *Consequently* shows that something is the result of something and synonyms would be *therefore, thus, as a result* or *in consequence*. *Subsequently* is a time adverbial and a synonym would be *later on* or *afterwards*.
6 a) why   b) for   c) on   d) in
e) In … with   f) In … to   g) to
h) In   i) from
7 When making a final point after several other points have been made. It serves to emphasise that it may be the last point being made but it is not the least important.

12 1 a) *I was impressed by the quality of the service provided* is the first point which the writer wants to make about the hotel.

b) The writer had a good first impression of the quality of the service but the implication is that later she changed her mind.

2 a) *It has a swimming pool and other sports facilities* is the last point in a list of points made about the hotel.
b) It has – after some years of waiting – now got a swimming pool. (A synonym for *at last* here would be *eventually*.)
c) The implication is that there is not much else good about the hotel, apart from its swimming pool and other sports facilities.

3 a) The supplier probably does not yet know about the proposed location but someone else is imagining how the supplier would feel about it.
b) The supplier thinks that the location is inconvenient.

4 a) *Its spaciousness is very attractive* is a point which contrasts with a previous point made which was negative about the hotel in some way, e.g. *Its decor is rather old-fashioned*.
b) *Its spaciousness is very attractive* is contradicting something said previously by someone else who felt its spaciousness was ugly.

5 a) *It is within easy reach of the capital* is an additional point made after at least one other good point about the hotel.
b) *It is within easy reach of the capital* is contrasting with a previously made negative point.
c) *It is within easy reach of the capital* is drawing a logical conclusion from other points made about the hotel's location, e.g. *It is very close to both a railway station and the M11*.

6 a) *As far as we are concerned* just gives emphasis to the point that the writer is writing only about her own organisation's requirements and is not considering requirements other people might have.
b) The writer is unsure and worried as to whether the hotel would satisfy their requirements or not.

13 1 a) is not very good because the string of short sentences does not read very well. b) is much better as it combines the points made into much more well constructed sentences.

2 a) is better because it is much more specific both about the proportions of participants who were dissatisfied and about what the exact problems were.

3 b) is much better than a) in that it uses a much wider range of vocabulary. The use of *good* in a) is not only repetitive and, therefore, poor style, it also does not show the examiner much about the student's knowledge of vocabulary.

4 The texts here are identical but a) will get a better mark than b) because it is clear to read. The handwriting is legible and any corrections have been made in a tidy way.

14 All these points will help you to keep corrections to a minimum and, when they are necessary, to make them neatly.

– Spend plenty of time planning before you start writing.
– Think carefully as you write – about endings and spellings of difficult words, for example.
– Write on alternate lines.
– Use reasonably large handwriting.
– Make corrections by putting one line through the error and then writing the correction clearly above the crossing out.

– Alternatively, use correcting fluid but make sure your correction is dry before you write over it.

Unit 7   Writing about work

1

Task	Text type required	Content of task	Target reader	Style required
2	letter	description of programme for week's visit; explanation of why activities on the programme are (a) interesting and (b) useful	foreign colleague	must be consistent but could be formal or informal
3	report	description of possible location in home area for fast food outlet – comments regarding market, competition, availability of workers, transport for materials and customers and any other relevant factors; concluding recommendation	managers of company from another country	formal
4	magazine article	brief description of job, recommend (or otherwise) and give advice on training and how to succeed	teenagers at school	neutral / informal

2
1. Hospital, operating theatre – theatre, pass over scalpels, swabs, scrub up
2. Office – board meeting, take the minutes, do shorthand
3. Department store – cosmetics, turnover, range, stock
4. Farm – fertilisers, crops, gather in the harvest
5. University / college – freshers, tutor, Societies Fair, Students' Union, term

4 Time: as, before, hardly, no sooner, since, the moment, until, when, whenever, while, whilst
Condition: as long as, if, provided, supposing, unless,
Purpose: in order not to, in order that, in order to, so as to, so that, to
Reason: as, because, in case, since
Manner: as, as if, as though, just as, like
Concession: although, despite the fact that, even though, much as, whereas, while, whilst

5
1. No sooner   2. The moment   3. Hardly
4. as though   5. provided   6. in case
7. in order to   8. despite the fact that

6 Some possible answers are suggested below.

1. I became a politician in order to *play my part in improving social conditions.*
2. He has detested his boss since *the moment he was first introduced to him.*
3. She enjoys her work although *she would prefer not to have to commute every day.*
4. James got a good job in a bank whereas *Bill is still travelling around Australia.*
5. The new employee walked into the office as if *the company belonged to him.*
6. Jim has a coffee break whenever *he feels like it.*
7. I'll accept the job as long as *the pay they offer is reasonable.*
8. I wouldn't consider working for him – much as *I need to find a job.*

7 2 comparing, pointing to similarities (the same way, similarly)

3 contrasting (alternatively, conversely, nonetheless, on the contrary)

4 expressing the idea of a result (as a result, consequently)

5 coming to a conclusion (all things considered, to conclude)

6 giving an opinion (as far as I am concerned, to my mind)

7 providing order for points in a list (lastly, thirdly)

8 giving an idea of time (beforehand, before long, immediately, suddenly, within an hour)

9 expressing the idea that something has taken or seems to have taken a very long time to happen (finally)

8 1 The odd one out is C. It does not make sense in this context. It could be used to link the following sentences: *It was a good thing that Janet was a trained nurse. Otherwise, grandma might have died.*

2 The odd one out is C. It makes sense in this context but it gives a slightly different impression than the other options. It suggests that the speaker has taken a long slow look at the reasons why Tolstoy can be considered a great novelist and has stated these in detail in the preceding lecture or article. A and B, on the other hand, merely present this point as the concluding one (which probably, but not inevitably, follows on from what has been stated previously).

3 A is the odd one out although it could make sense in this context. It simply makes it clear that this was the last in a series of events whereas the others emphasise the point that finding a job took or seemed to take a long time.

4 B is the odd one out although it can certainly make sense in the context. It is relating the situation to the speaker's own position whereas the other adverbials indicate that the speaker is giving his or her own opinion and we know nothing about whether the speaker is personally practically affected by what he or she is commenting on.

5 The odd one out is C although it can again fit in this context. It implies that Michael is a strong candidate for the same reason as Katie

is (perhaps they've both been in the company for a long time, for example) whereas the other three simply say that they are both good candidates and this may be for very different reasons.

9 These are the more formal alternatives.

1 a) whilst
  b) so as to
  c) in order to / in order that
  d) no sooner

2 a) furthermore
  b) equally
  c) by contrast
  d) thus
  e) subsequently

10 These are the most likely positions for the various adverbials listed. They may occasionally occur in other places as well.

1 Salaries are good in the company. *At the same time / Besides / Furthermore / Moreover* they *also* have an excellent career structure *as well / on top of that / too.*

2 Valerie is an excellent typist. *Again / Equally / In the same way / Likewise / Similarly* she is first-rate at shorthand.

3 We could promote Mary. *Alternatively* we could promote her husband *instead.* She is very good at her job. *By contrast,* Jim is not efficient at all. *However / Nevertheless / Nonetheless / On the other hand,* he is more popular.

4 A: Mary is very good at her job.
  B: *On the contrary,* she's very disorganised.

5 We must get started on the project. *Otherwise* we won't finish the job on time.

6 We were pleased with the company's work. *Accordingly / As a result / Consequently / So / Thus,* we shall, *therefore,* use them again.

7 *All things considered / In conclusion / To conclude / To sum up,* the project was an unqualified success.

8 *According to my mother / As far as I am concerned / As I see it / In my opinion / To my mind,* the redundancies should never have been made.
  Note that with *personally,* you need to say *Personally, I think / feel / believe that the redundancies should never have been made.*

9 *Appropriately enough / Luckily / Not surprisingly / Unfortunately*, Jim took over as manager when his uncle retired. *Broadly speaking / Significantly* he was, *certainly / surely*, his uncle's favourite nephew.
Note the change that needs to be made here: *Jim took over as manager when his uncle retired undoubtedly / chiefly / mainly / primarily because he was his uncle's favourite nephew.*

10 *Firstly / Last but not least / Lastly / Next / Secondly / Thirdly*, the level of unemployment is an important factor in crime.

11 Jack jumped into the pool *at first / beforehand / immediately. Then / Afterwards / Before long / Subsequently / Suddenly* Maria dived in *within an hour.*

12 I waited for the bus. *At last / Finally* it *eventually* arrived.

11 Some possible answers are suggested below.

1 I'll finish the sales report <u>when / as soon as</u> I get home.
2 <u>Because / Since / As</u> she has an important position in the company, she gets an excellent salary.
3 Correct.
4 She worked very hard. <u>Despite that / All the same / Nevertheless</u>, she got the sack.
5 Correct.
6 Jane graduated from university with a first class honours degree in Spanish. Jill, <u>likewise</u>, has very good qualifications.
7 <u>As far as the management is concerned</u>, he is the perfect employee. His colleagues, <u>however</u>, know that he is extremely lazy.
8 She did very well at the interview and was, <u>consequently</u>, offered the position <u>provided that</u> she agreed to do a typing course one evening a week.

12 Some possible answers are suggested below.

1 Firstly   2 as a result   3 Next
4 consequently   5 Moreover   6 Finally
7 eventually   8 However   9 Fortunately

13 1 Not effective because it does not come to a firm conclusion.
2 Leaves the reader with a very negative final impression. The writer should have organised his or her time better.

3 Not good because the language is inaccurate; it should read *I would suggest <u>opening</u> a Chips Palace in Cae-on-Sea <u>for</u> the reasons I <u>gave</u> above.*
4 Very poor. It seems to criticise the examiners, which is a bit risky.
5 A good concrete proposal in accurate and effective language.
6 Far too informal in style.
7 Very good.
8 Inaccurate. It should read <u>To conclude</u> / <u>All things considered</u>, *I think you should <u>go</u> ahead with the project. Otherwise, you could miss out on a golden <u>opportunity</u>.* Even when written correctly it is not as good as 5 or 7. The last phrase is a little informal for most reports and the two introductory phrases are a little repetitive – it would be better to use either one or the other.

Unit 8   Notes, notices and announcements

1 Brevity, clarity and precision are particularly appropriate for the writing of notes, notices and announcements. The other characteristics are not usually appropriate.

2 1 Not precise enough about what was left.
2 Not brief enough. Too much that is irrelevant.
3 Not clear enough. Writer should have organised thoughts before setting them down on paper. Also it is not brief enough.
4 Not clear enough in presentation of information – order of information, layout and amount of detail provided could all be improved.
5 Doesn't specify what books are for sale. Doesn't give telephone number.

3 The advice is all valid for writing notes, notices and announcements.

4 1 Name of film, date, time, where to be shown and (perhaps) cost of ticket
2 Where going, when, request for fellow-traveller, cost
3 Can't go, reason, apology, name

5 1 Thursday, Please ring doctor as soon as possible

2 bicycle, 28 inches (approximately 63 centimetres), or nearest offer

3 furnished, bedrooms, reception rooms, kitchen and bathroom, central heating, situation, professional man or woman, per calendar month

4 Very Important Person's expected time of arrival, hours, meeting, head of department, departure, headquarters

5 Terrace, Wednesday, October, Répondez s'il vous plaît (reply, please), Bring your own bottle

6 information, John F. Kennedy, pages, third volume, encyclopaedia, problems, library assistant

6 1 Putting the word *friend* into inverted commas makes it clear that the person is a friend in name only.

2 a) The writer has a number of brothers. We know which one is being talked about because of the defining clause *who lives in London*.

b) The writer has only one brother. The fact that he lives in London is just an extra piece of information about him.

3 a) The exclamation mark shows that the speaker is surprised by the news he or she is passing on.

b) The question mark emphasises that the person cannot believe that what he or she is hearing can be true. He or she is asking for confirmation.

4 a) More than one cat had kittens.
b) One cat had kittens.

5 The capital letters for *Good Thing* create a humorous effect. They imply, perhaps, that the person writing about it does not take the remarks very seriously.

6 a) Bombs should be dropped whether there is an attack or not.

b) Bombs should not be dropped unless there is attack.

7 a) The writer and his or her friends or possibly some people the writer knew were really excited by the news the person has told them.

b) The writer and his or her friends are really excited by the fact that the person they are speaking to has made news headlines.

8 a) The question is about a person, the woman married to Sam.

b) The question is about a film or a book.

7 A

I'd love to go out with you and Sally on Tues. night. Let's meet in the Red Lion on Bridge St. at 8 and then go, if we can get tickets, to the concert in the Town Hall. The Rocky Horrors are playing. Have you heard of them? I hadn't until a couple of weeks ago when Jane took me to her cousin's house and he was raving about them.

They're a new English group. Apparently, they're really popular abroad already, especially with French and Japanese kids. They had a smash hit in the States with 'Let's Tango in Paris' which almost got into the Top Ten here too. It's pretty good, if you don't object to a Heavy Metal beat. Anyhow, we can hear for ourselves next week, if you agree.

I'll give you a ring on Sun. to see what you think.
Love,
Harriet

B
Arts Cinema, Cambridge
Mon. 27 and Tue. 28 Dec.
Singing, Ringing Tree
A beautiful and haughty princess is tamed by a beast and a magic tree. A rare treat for all those thirty-somethings who saw this East German classic on the television in the 60's. It will charm the new generation too.

8 1 writing   2 foreign   3 professor
4 Wednesday   5 government   6 science
7 especially   8 medicine   9 psychiatry
10 pronunciation   11 difficult
12 language   13 skilful   14 referred
15 fascinating   16 research   17 Brazil
18 recommended   19 February
20 address   21 secretary   22 committee
23 application   24 offered
25 arguments   26 relevance
27 scientists   28 embarrassed
29 together   30 separate

10 1 raise   2 practice
3 lose, chance / opportunity   4 wear
5 lie / stay
6 experiments, experiences, interested

Unit 9 Instructions and directions

1 – The instructions are not in the most logical order, e.g. *You have to get a six before you can start playing* would have been better said earlier on.
  – They are inaccurate at times, e.g. *The first person to get to the end* – rather than the beginning – *is the winner*.
  – They are not always precise enough, e.g. it does not say what happens if you land at the head end of a snake.

2 h j e i g d b k a c f

3 1 Safety when water-skiing
  Needs and rules
  What skis are like
  Practice on shore: putting on your skis
  Practice on shore: taking up the crouching position
  Practice on shore: practice with the tow-bar
  Starting on water
  Moving in the water
  Stopping in the water

  2 The first phrase gives a precise measurement.
  The second phrase describes something in a specific way.
  The third phrase uses precise verbs.

  3 precise times and measurements – 48 kph, between one hour after sunset and one hour before sunrise, 1,700 mm
  precise verbs – wet, hold down, slip, pull up, crouch, extend, grasp, idle, accelerate, rise, plane, release
  precisely defined objects – approved water-ski safety jacket, approved tow-rope, general purpose skis for beginners, waist-deep water
  reasons for doing something – first sentence

4 Here are some possible answers.

  1 Leave the marinated meat to soak for 6 to 8 hours.
  2 Cut an equilateral triangle, with 5 cm. sides, out of a piece of strong paper.
  3 Every three months top up the anti-freeze so that the engine continues to run smoothly throughout the year.
  4 Chop the vegetables into bite-sized pieces before cooking.

  5 Begin the exercise routine by lying on your back on the floor with your arms straight down by your sides, palms on the ground.

5 The following instructions would, probably, be better corrected along the lines suggested below.

  – Avoid taking stimulants – a cup of coffee, for example – shortly before going to bed.
  – Do not have a substantial meal just before you go to bed.
  – A brisk walk just before you go to bed can help you sleep.
  – Warm milk at bedtime can help you sleep.
  – A soft mattress can prevent sleep – something slightly harder is usually more restful.
  – We usually imagine counting sheep rather than polar bears but there is no reason why polar bears would not be just as effective.

6 1 B 2 C 3 A 4 C 5 D
  6 D 7 C 8 A

8 1 Using a bank cashpoint machine.
  2 Being introduced to someone.
  3 Invisible writing (read by holding up to a warm light bulb or gently ironing).
  4 What to do with houseplants when you go on holiday.
  5 Making meringue.

9 Here are some possible ways of rewording these instructions. There are many others.

  2 – On being introduced to someone you should stand up, if you were sitting, and should shake hands.
    – When you are introduced to someone, it is considered good manners to stand up, if you are sitting, and to shake hands.

  3 – It is possible to use bottled or squeezed lemon juice or the juice from a grated onion. Try dipping a toothpick into the juice and writing on hard-surfaced paper.
    – Good results can be obtained by dipping a toothpick into either bottled or freshly squeezed lemon juice or the juice from a grated onion. You would then be well advised to use hard-surfaced paper for writing on.

  4 – I recommend that you should move all your pots into a cool room where they will be away from direct sunlight.

– It is only sensible to move all your pots into a cool room so that they are away from direct sunlight.

5 – After whisking two egg whites in a bowl until stiff, add 50 g. of caster sugar and continue whisking until the mixture will stand in soft peaks and keeps its shape.

– The first thing to do is to whisk two egg whites in a bowl until stiff. When this is done, you should add 50 g. of caster sugar and should continue whisking until the mixture will stand in soft peaks and keeps its shape.

10 The directions are reasonably clear but they are not very well-expressed. The structures are very repetitive.

Unit 10   Reviews

1 A review should show all the things listed in 3.

2 1 The subject of the review is a new series of TV programmes based on videos produced by children.

The following facts are given in the review.
– Kerry Dunn, aged 12, made a short, home-made video called 'Life Without Dad' which is part of BBC2's new series of films, *As Seen on TV*.
– This is the first time such programmes have been made.
– Eric Rowan and Chris Morris, of children's BBC, wanted to give children what Morris calls a 'chance to tell their own truth'.
– They looked for children interested in making videos and lent them camcorders.
– The smaller children were occasionally chaperoned but basically the videos were made totally by the children themselves without adult intervention. They interview their families, talk alone in their bedrooms to tripod cameras.
– One of the films is about a blind boy and how he sees the world. In another some surfers put their point of view in Scotland, an orphan in Brighton talks about living with grandparents, and in one of the more violent films, which is later in the series, two 12-year-old girls made a documentary on the horrors of having to share a bedroom.

– The tapes were edited by Chris Morris who sent a rough-cut for approval by the child, tidied it up, and prepared it for showing.

2 Her opinion is very positive although she does admit that the content is uneven, occasionally even silly. The main way she conveys her positive feelings is through the enthusiasm with which she describes the programmes and their contents. The following phrases convey her opinion:
carries a lot more power, conviction and dignity than any politician has yet … startling highspot … herein lies the dignity … It was about time … one of the more violent films … The results are uneven, sometimes funny, sometimes passionate or silly. … for once nobody is patronising them.

3 She recommends that viewers do watch the programmes. She captures readers' interest in the series, telling them enough about it to arouse interest – but not too much so that they already know everything.

4 They would probably feel pleased by the publicity their series is given in this article. The reviewer is most specific about the positive parts of the series which would probably please those involved in its production.

5 This is a matter of opinion but it is certainly true to say that the writer makes a general point at the end of the review which does have a wider relevance than just the subject of the review, i.e. the point that television is just a 'medium for communication' which is potentially available to everyone and so should not hold any special mystique. She is also perhaps making a point about society's attitudes to children and how they have very little control over their lives.

3 Here are possible answers to these questions but there may well be others.

1 – Teenagers are a potentially interesting subject for a TV programme.
  – The writer has used humour – describing teenagers as if they were animals being observed in a nature programme.
2 – *Live Like Pigs* is still relevant today in the questions it poses about society.
  – Interest is aroused by the use of questions.
3 – Whitney Houston is a powerful singer.
  – The writer has compared her to

Schwarzenegger and used the metaphor of relating her voice to macho muscles.

4 1 A mixed metaphor which makes the situation sound ridiculous. The writer would have been better to say *As soon as he started to speak, he realised he had been tactless.*

2 A hanging participle. It isn't John's clothes which jump out of bed but it sounds as if it is.

3 This makes it sound as if she will be addressing the directors' meeting from the bath. It would be correct, one presumes, to put the participle phrase first – *Lying in the bath, she planned … .*

4 Repetitive. Find a different word for *interesting* and / or *interested*, for example, *I was fascinated by the spectacular views … .*

5 Misrelated participle. It should read *Born in 1976, he spent his childhood in London.*

6 The honest truth is an example of a 'tautology'. The truth is, by definition, *honest* and so the word *honest* is redundant.

7 Something cannot be *very unique* or, for that matter, *quite unique*. Something is either unique or it isn't.

8 Mixed metaphor. You wouldn't expect anything concrete to come from an olive branch. It would be better to complete the sentence … *but it was not accepted.*

6 Positive words

brilliant	captivating	dynamic
engrossing	exhilarating	fascinating
first-rate	impressive	inspiring
invaluable	stimulating	tasteful

Negative words

absurd	disgraceful	grotesque
irritating	ludicrous	self-conscious
self-indulgent	shameful	tedious

7 2 singer, positive
3 film, positive
4 restaurant, negative
5 TV programme, positive
6 painting, positive
7 poetry, both positive and negative aspects here
8 play, both positive and negative aspects here too

9 1 to   2 In   3 with   4 concerned
5 As   6 view   7 opinion   8 speaking

10 These are the most likely combinations.

2 excruciatingly boring
3 deeply disappointing
4 eagerly awaited
5 admirably honest
6 considerably improved
7 impeccably dressed
8 richly deserved
9 perfectly formed
10 highly developed
11 wildly exciting

Unit 11   Brochures

1 a) 1 brochure
2 information sheet
3 leaflet
4 pamphlet

b) 1 information about at least three of the following – landscape; local food and drink; leisure facilities; places of historical interest; transport in your local area
2 where home is, its facilities, whom it would suit
3 basic details about the club, how to join, advantages of membership past activities
4 what the issue is and your opinion on it

c) 1 to visit the area (foreign tourists)
2 to come and stay in your home (if people of suitable type)
3 join the club
4 agree with your point of view

2 1 The brochure provides information about three tourist sights in London.
2 It is trying to attract people to visit these sights.
3 All of the bottom part of each section is giving information. There is also information in the top part but it is also mixed up with sales talk.
4 The writer uses a number of techniques: pictures; addressing the reader directly, by using *you* and imperatives; vivid vocabulary to make the places sound attractive; lists, e.g. *Lights … Camera … Action* and the sentence beginning *Enjoy a magic lantern show … .* The sentences tend to contain a lot of adjectives and try to pack in as much information as possible without becoming too long and complex.
5 There are many words and expressions you

could underline here. For example, from MOMI – *award-winning, fascinating, magical, exciting blend, hands-on fun, enjoy, encourage participation*; from Tower Hill Pageant – *relive, complementing, exciting discoveries, most fascinating attractions*; from Science Museum – *many thousands of objects, world-famous collections, exciting combination, special events, popular, made ... history, encourage, hands-on, interactive*, You may well be able to justify underlining others.

3 1 True. But it is not necessary to present your work like this if you don't want to.
2 True.
3 False. How you draw is irrelevant in an English exam.
4 False. It will certainly make it look authentic but it won't impress the examiner unless your English is good and so it is better to spend valuable time concentrating on your use of language.
5 False. What is being tested is your ability to handle brochure English. If you write good text in appropriate paragraphs, possibly under different headings, then it does not matter if you do not pay attention to visual aspects of your work.
6 It depends. Using different coloured pens may make you feel more as if you are doing an authentic task and it will certainly create a good impression. It shouldn't take much extra time – if it does, it is not worth the effort.
7 False. You could waste a lot of time making sure that your information is complete and accurate. Just give enough of such information to give a satisfactory answer to the task but don't worry about the accuracy or the completeness of the 'facts' you present in the exam.

4 1 catchy slogan; imperative; addressing the reader personally
2 exaggeration; addressing the reader personally; promise of a bargain
3 addressing the reader personally; promise of a bargain
4 question (rhetorical); addressing the reader personally
5 exaggeration; pictures in words; addressing the reader personally; imperatives; adjectives
6 question; addressing the reader personally
7 example of personal experience

8 addressing the reader personally; pictures in words; adjectives; exaggeration

6 The words and expressions that you might find particularly useful are listed below. You may have chosen others as well.

1 Don't miss
2 couldn't be simpler; the heart of the capital
3 Whether you are ... simply off to see the sights; the ... for you; the further ... the better; very popular
4 to get away from it all
5 the world's greatest ... adventure; the real; magical; discover the sights and sounds; fascinating; leading experts; explore
6 tell you more about
7 It's time
8 ancient; unruffled charm; as long ago as; fascinating legacy; beautiful and historic; elegant; secret; unchanged for hundreds of years

7 1 Idioms are most widely used in speech and informal writing.
2 The most likely text types to include idioms are: letters (informal ones); articles (in popular magazines); narratives (in dialogues); notes, notices and announcements; instructions and directions (informal ones); brochures.
3 Idioms are often found, for example, in horoscopes, in advertisements, in answers to letters on magazine or newspaper problem pages.

8 1 A   2 C   3 B
4 D   5 A   6 C
7 C   8 D

9 1 off the beaten <u>track</u>
2 <u>do</u> justice to
3 the <u>tip</u> of the iceberg
4 <u>scratch</u> the surface
5 once in <u>a</u> blue moon
6 <u>dance</u> attendance
7 kill two birds with one <u>stone</u>
8 on the spur of the <u>moment</u>
9 live <u>up</u> to your expectations
10 letting the cat out of <u>the</u> bag
11 <u>pull</u> out all the stops
12 lets the grass grow under our <u>feet</u>

10 The twenty errors are underlined and corrected below.

I am <u>writting</u> this leaflet because I want <u>that</u> <u>everyone know</u> what a wonderful town I live in. Not many people <u>lives</u> here and so it is a <u>quite</u> and peaceful place. Many visitors come here <u>for</u> <u>relax</u> and recover after an illness.

Many famous people <u>visited</u> this town. For example, Julia Roberts, David Copperfield and Elizabeth Taylor <u>have all come</u> here last year. They were feeling <u>badly</u> when they arrived but they soon stopped <u>to feel</u> ill here.

The town is surrounded <u>with</u> high mountains and you can <u>breath</u> a <u>wonderful fresh air</u>. If you feel fit, you can rent a <u>bycicle</u> and go for a ride into the mountains. If you <u>will come</u> in winter, you will be able to <u>skiing</u>.

Some people may wonder what <u>is there</u> to do in the evenings in <u>a such</u> small town. But there are several fine restaurants and clubs and the night-life is really <u>unexpected</u> good.

We are looking forward to <u>see</u> you when you <u>will come</u> to visit us.

The corrections are listed below.

writing	everyone to know	live
quiet	to relax	have visited
all came	bad	feeling by
breathe	wonderful fresh air	
bicycle	come	go skiing or ski
there is	such a	unexpectedly
seeing	come	

Unit 12   Competition entries

1

1 article (Unit 4)
2 narrative (Unit 5)
3 article (Unit 4)
4 article or report (Unit 4 or 6) This task also involves writing about work so Unit 7 will help as well.

2

Task	Who are you writing for?	What are you expected to cover?
1	judges, probably journalists, selected by a young people's magazine	where to go to do a report; what to report; who to interview; what to ask them
2	judges, probably students, selected by an international student magazine	something to do with being a student; something relevant to today and possibly something with an international element
3	judges selected by a newspaper	which charity you would choose; why; how the money might be spent
4	judges from your own workplace, mainly your own bosses	qualities of good and bad bosses; some examples from own experience; advice; you as a boss

5 Here are some possible answers.

1 I would take a tape recorder to the interview in case *I wasn't able to take shorthand quickly enough.*

2 As long as *I didn't have to keep the books myself*, I think I'd make a good boss.

3 No sooner *had he* arrived at the college *than he bumped into the girl he had met at his interview.*

4 I would make an excellent boss although *I am not sure I would enjoy being one.*

5 My first boss was very difficult to work for whereas *the second one was the perfect boss.*

6 My current boss works as if *his only interest in life is his work.*

7 My current boss works like *a horse.* (i.e. a noun or noun phrase making a comparison)

8 I would donate the money to research into cancer despite the fact that *a cure for cancer is many years away.*

9 A good boss means that employees enjoy their work more. Moreover, *they are likely to work harder for a sympathetic boss.*

10 I would give my money to medical research. Eventually *a cure will be found for many of the illnesses we most fear today and I should like to do my bit to help that day come more quickly.*

11 I should very much like to interview Arnold Schwarzenegger. However, *he does not often agree to give interviews.*

12 I think the money should go towards research into heart disease. Alternatively, *it could usefully be spent on finding a cure for cancer.*

13 Jack is good at dealing with people but not very efficient with his correspondence. Milly, conversely, *is efficient with her correspondence but poor at dealing with people.*

14 She was very successful as deputy manager. As a result, *she was instantly promoted to manager on Mr Smith's retirement.*

7 Here are twelve possible phrases. You can undoubtedly justify the inclusion of others.

all's well that ends well   all things considered
finally   in conclusion   last but not least
lastly   lived happily ever after
look forward to hearing from you
to come to the conclusion that   to conclude
to sum up   would certainly recommend

8 1 These sentences are all short and simple and they sound very flat and monotonous. It would be better to say, for instance: *Having woken up early, I couldn't go back to sleep. So I got dressed and went for a walk. There was no-one else about.*

2 This text repeats the basic second conditional structure a number of times. It would be better to vary it somewhat. Make sure that you are aware of all the different possibilities here as competition entries often require you to make hypothetical statements of this kind. You could say:
If I won the competition, I would buy a new car. Should there be any money left over, I would spend it on travel. I would enjoy travelling more were I to go with someone else. So supposing there wasn't too much money left over, I would spend it on a holiday for two somewhere nearby rather than go somewhere more exotic on my own.

3 The phrase *made mistakes* is used in a very repetitive way. It would be better to say, for instance: *I made a lot of mistakes when I first started learning English. My grammar was weak, of course, and I misspelt lots of words. But I had most problems of all with pronunciation.*

4 It would be possible to demonstrate your range of vocabulary by being more precise about the furniture in the room. You could say: *The room was very crowded with three armchairs and a long sofa as well as a large mahogany sideboard and two modern coffee tables.*

5 This text uses a lot of weak words, e.g. *nice, good, beautiful.* You could show off a bit and say: *Edinburgh is a very enjoyable place to visit. It's a magnificent city with lots of fascinating places to see and there are varied and exciting things to do in the evening too.*

6 Again, here is a chance to demonstrate a range of vocabulary. For example: *There was a lot to see from the windows as the train travelled through the country – long low farm-houses, enormous fields of wheat and maize and the occasional tower of a church in the distance.*

9 1 The word *shoot* is highly ambiguous and would be better as *film* or *photograph.*

2 This sounds as though all 12,500 are in one cell. It would be worded better as *are having to live in shared cells.*

3 The expression *floating voters* (people who

sometimes vote for one party and sometimes for a different one) sounds humorous in the context of a discussion of coastal waters. It would be better to say *Voters uncertain of their allegiance* or something along those lines.

4 The word *poach* can mean either to take fish, animals or birds illegally from someone else's land or to cook eggs (without their shells) in water. Therefore, the sentence is humorously ambiguous. It would be better perhaps to say *A man has been questioned in connection with their theft.*

5 Again, two meanings of a word make this sound probably accidentally funny. *Post* can mean *send a letter, or greetings card, through the post* or it can mean *be sent to work somewhere*. It might be better to say here that *Lloyd has been sent to work*.

6 *Escaped* makes it sound as if the boys were in a cage at the Zoo. *Were unhurt* might sound better.

7 This is ambiguous as *toasted* can mean cooked over heat or drank the health of. It would be better to say *the guests drank to the health and happiness of the couple*, perhaps.

8 *Get the group off the ground* is not the best idiom to use here as it is easy to imagine bell-ringers being hoisted up into the air by the ropes they have to pull. *Get the group started* would be better in this context.

Acknowledgements

The author would like to thank Jeanne McCarten, Lindsay White, Liz Sharman and Liz Driscoll who all did so much work on this project. Thanks are also due to the many helpful readers, whose contributions were so productive. Of these, particular mention should go to Paul Carne.

The author and the publisher are grateful to the following individuals and institutions for permission to reproduce copyright material. It has not been possible to identify the sources of all the material used and in such cases the publishers would welcome information from copyright holders.

p. 36 (1) extract from 'Motherhood past midnight' by David Concar, Andy Coghlan and Phillida Brown, reproduced by permission of *New Scientist*, (2) extract from 'Jungle stories', reproduced by permission of *BBC Wildlife Magazine*, (3) extract from 'A flexible society that would let us work, rest and play' by Patricia Hewlett, *The Guardian*, (4) extract from 'Chorus of disapproval for English curriculum' by Colin Hughes, *The Independent*; p. 72 'Orange to Apple' and p.73 'Waterskiing' from *How to do just about anything – 1988*, reproduced by permission of *Readers Digest*; p. 80 extracts from 'Vision' by Peter Barnard and 'Welfare States' by John Peter and p. 81 extract by Robert Sandall, reproduced by permission of Times Newspapers Limited; p. 81 extract from *Usage and Abusage* by Eric Partridge, reproduced by permission of Hamish Hamilton Ltd; p. 87 and p.89 extracts from *British Rail Brochures*.

For permission to reproduce photographs: Robert Harding Picture Library (p. 35, p. 37 fisherman, p. 37 barbecue, p. 73, p. 84 cinema, p. 89 no.1); The Image Bank (p. 37 cocktail by pool, p. 89 no.4); Tony Stone Images (p. 37 couple, p. 57 surgeons, p. 57 perfume counter, p. 57 meeting); Sygma (p. 81 left, p. 81 right); The Hutchison Library (p. 84 top); Milepost 92$^{1/2}$ (p. 89 no.3, p. 89 no.6); Barnaby's Picture Library (p. 89 no.8). Other photography by Jeremy Pembrey.

Text artwork by Paul Dickinson: pp. 27, 28, 33, 42; Amanda MacPhail: pp. 9, 74, 75, 98; Bill Piggins: pp. 61, 72; Tess Stone: p. 71.

Thanks are due to Peter Ducker for his design assistance.